REAL KIDS DON'T SAY PLEASE

REAL KIDS DON'T SAY PLEASE

April and Dan Levy

Illustrated by Paul Harrington

STEIN AND DAY/*Publishers*/New York

First published in 1984.
Text Copyright © 1984 by April and Dan Levy
Illustrations Copyright © 1984
  by Stein and Day, Incorporated
Designed by Louis A. Ditizio
Printed in the United States of America
STEIN AND DAY/*Publishers*
Scarborough House
Briarcliff Manor, N.Y. 10510

Library of Congress Cataloging in Publication Data

Levy, April.
  Real Kids don't say please.

  1. Children—Anecdotes, facetiae, satire, etc.
2. Children—Miscellanea.   I. Levy, Dan.   II. Title.
HQ767.9.L48   1984   305.2'3   83-40352
ISBN 0-8128-6219-8 (pbk.)

To Morris Eli, our Real Kid

Contents

REAL KIDS DON'T SAY PLEASE

1

INTRODUCTION

This is a book about Real Kids—the kind of kid no parent wants to admit to having and no adult wants to admit to having been.

Real Kids, on the other hand, readily confess to being Real Kids. They wouldn't have it any other way. They enjoy the shudder they evoke in shopkeepers as they pass tightly by a display tower of crystal stemware or the look of disgust the class brain shoots at their rumpled homework papers. Real Kids like being Real Kids. No fooling.

Real Kids generally run between five and thirteen—old enough to have secrets but not to keep them; old enough to be supposed to go to school and too young to convince anybody they're there when they aren't. They're at the age when birthdays are still fun—for them anyway. After all, the only thing better than being an eleven year-old Real Kid is being a twelve-year old Real Kid. To the Real Kid, that is.

Of course, some Real Kids never grow up. They go quietly gray, still ogling offers on cereal boxes for baking-powder-powered atomic submarines, magic sets, and glow-in-the-dark bicycle plates with their name on them. The thing that distinguishes big Real Kids from the standard variety is that they don't have to ask anybody when they want a Ball Park hot dog, Captain Crunch, or a 12-ounce bag of Tootsie Roll Midgies.

Real Kids are what you always think *other* people's kids are, and what you try to convince yourself yours aren't. They are not at all like kids used to be—or anyway like you used to be—or anyway not much.

How do you recognize Real Kids? Easy!

Let the brave read on.

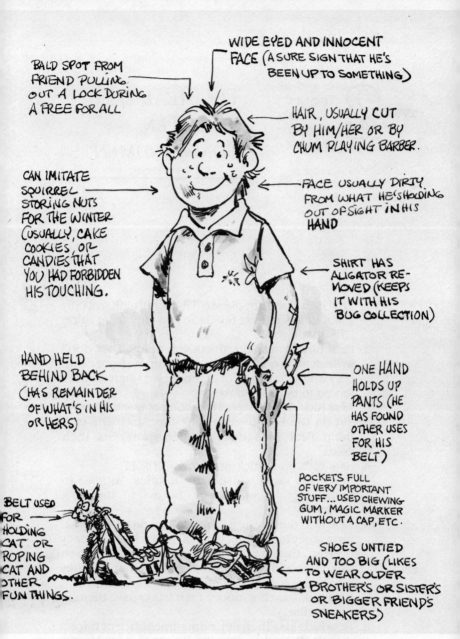

BALD SPOT FROM FRIEND PULLING OUT A LOCK DURING A FREE FOR ALL

WIDE EYED AND INNOCENT FACE (A SURE SIGN THAT HE'S BEEN UP TO SOMETHING)

HAIR, USUALLY CUT BY HIM/HER OR BY CHUM PLAYING BARBER.

CAN IMITATE SQUIRREL STORING NUTS FOR THE WINTER (USUALLY, CAKE COOKIES, OR CANDIES THAT YOU HAD FORBIDDEN HIS TOUCHING.

FACE USUALLY DIRTY FROM WHAT HE'S HOLDING OUT OF SIGHT IN HIS HAND

SHIRT HAS ALIGATOR REMOVED (KEEPS IT WITH HIS BUG COLLECTION)

HAND HELD BEHIND BACK (HAS REMAINDER OF WHAT'S IN HIS OR HERS)

ONE HAND HOLDS UP PANTS (HE HAS FOUND OTHER USES FOR HIS BELT)

POCKETS FULL OF VERY IMPORTANT STUFF... USED CHEWING GUM, MAGIC MARKER WITHOUT A CAP, ETC.

BELT USED FOR HOLDING CAT OR ROPING CAT AND OTHER FUN THINGS.

SHOES UNTIED AND TOO BIG (LIKES TO WEAR OLDER BROTHER'S OR SISTER'S OR BIGGER FRIEND'S SNEAKERS)

Can be used to check off your own Real Kid's description and add the unique things he or she has.

2

THE REAL KIDS' TEN COMMANDMENTS

---

1. Real Kids don't say please. They say thank you only when their mothers tell them in a menacing voice: "Say thank you."
2. Real Kids don't write thank-you notes. They don't write at all to relatives. They write home from camp only when they run out of money, or when they are forced to by the counselor.
3. Real Kids don't share. They don't play with the new kid on the block—unless he has Atari. The only thing Real Kids do share—invariably—is their colds.
4. Real Kids don't trick-or-treat for UNICEF.
5. Real Kids don't whisper in libraries. Within two minutes of being told to "be quiet," they talk louder.
6. Real Kids don't return library books on time. Sometimes they lose them. When a library book is really overdue, they may tell the librarian they lost it even when they didn't because they think that way they won't have to pay the fine.
7. Real Kids lose the money their father gave them to pay the fine.
8. Real Kids lose their key, sometimes once or twice a month. Then they lose the key their mother gave them to use temporarily.

9. Real Kids don't do their homework as soon as they get home from school. They forget to get notices signed. Real Kids don't save for their education.
10. Real Kids don't do anything they say they will "do later."
11.* Real Kids don't take candy from strange men—but they have to be real strange.

---

*Real Kids don't see why you can't have eleven commandments.

3

THE CARE AND MAINTENANCE OF REAL KIDS

Parental advice gets thrown around generously between the first time a kid wakes up dry and when he or she starts to wear a jock strap or use Tampax. Nine-tenths of it gets ignored, and it's about time parents faced the facts: Real Kids aren't Betty Anderson. They aren't even Bud Anderson. At best, by around eleven A.M. on a typical morning Real Kids resemble the Tide kid "before"—the one who's just got his shirt black with dirt, sliding headfirst into third. This is true even if they haven't yet left their room.

Today's parents are too hypertensive already to go worrying about whether their kids' shoes are shined. They should save their breath for stress tests and stop giving kids advice they won't take. Among the hard truths to be borne in mind are the following:

Real Kids don't use Kleenex. (Everybody knows what they *do* use.)

Real Kids don't brush after every meal. In fact, they might not brush at all if it weren't for mint toothpaste.

Real Kids wash with water and a towel—only.

Real Kids don't like baths and they hate head washes. Real Kids know that no-tears shampoo stings. They don't get their hair styled; most don't even get it cut when they can help it.

Real Kids don't use nail clippers. They don't have to.

This we call the kid's bathroom, but it's actually a toxic waste dump.

Real Kids don't change their socks every day and certainly not for a matching pair. They never put their dirty laundry in the hamper. In fact, it's not always possible to identify just what among a Real Kid's belongings *is* laundry.

Real Kids don't make their bed in the morning, and by afternoon they figure it'd be dumb to make something you're just going to mess up in a couple of hours.

Defying standard practice for other criminals, there's no need to call in the FBI to find the fingerprints a Real Kid has left at the scene of the crime; the fact is, when a Real Kid comes into the house, he doesn't entirely leave the outside behind.

Real Kids don't "bundle up." They don't button the top button. They don't wear galoshes. They don't carry umbrellas either, and they make fun of children who do. Real Kids don't wear anything over their ears except Walkman.

Real Kids scratch bites.

And they never get sick on weekends.

4

THREE THINGS REAL KIDS THINK IMPROVE WITH AGE

1. Chewing gum

2. Underpants

3. Halloween candy

5

THE REAL KIDS' HALL OF FAME: A WHO'S WHO AND WHO AIN'T

*I*t takes guts for a Real Kid to rise to the top. No one is out there waiting to give a presidential citation to somebody for filching a quarter to buy gum without first asking "please," or for not filching the quarter and filching the gum instead.

Yet, throughout history, stalwarts have risen from the relative obscurity that is too often the fate of the unsung heroes of video arcade and principal's office to live with us as Real Kids, even after their voices have changed and they've had to start using Clearasil.

Chief among these immortals are the Little Rascals. Through reels of *Our Gang* tapes, not one of this erstwhile crew was heard to utter "please." Spanky, Alfalfa, Buckwheat, Porky, Wheezer, Farina, Mary, and Stymie—all are to be counted among the rolls of Real Kiddom. So are the East Side Kids—urban urchins, some of whom managed to remain Real Kids right through puberty, male menopause, and the Bowery Boys.

And there are other Real Kids who have managed to strike the public fancy: Dennis the Menace became famous for not saying please. Annie didn't say it in 1938 or in 1983 either. Beaver Cleaver once asked Wally what it meant but never said it without being coerced by Ward or June. Real Kids all.

And then there were those big Real Kids of yesteryear: Stan Laurel and Oliver Hardy, Harpo Marx, Nikita Khrushchev (banging a shoe at the U.N. General Assembly earns him permanent Real-Kidnick status), John Belushi, Harry Truman, Pinky Lee. Babe Ruth was a Real Kid (the lucky stiff even got a candy bar named after him). Joe DiMaggio was too, but he forfeited his credentials when he became Mr. Coffee. George Washington might have been a Real Kid if he'd just eaten the cherries and kept his mouth shut. Lou Costello qualifies. Ditto Fiorello. Moe, Larry, Curly, and Shep are some of the Great Ones: Real Kids' Real Kids.

Of course, there have always been hordes of popularly celebrated please-sayers no one would mistake for Real Kids. Just look at the Quiz Kids. Art Linkletter wouldn't let anybody on his show who didn't say please: Real Kids were not among those who said the "darndest things" on "House Party."

Back in the fifties, Eddie Haskell said please whenever he spoke to Beaver's parents. And Lumpy Rutherford did too—except when the adult was his father. The Andersons taught all their children to say please—and only Bud refused. At least two of Fred MacMurray's sons said it, despite the influence of Tramp, Biff, and Uncle Charlie. The Lennon Sisters said please all the time to Mr. Welk. And Little Richie Petrie said it to Rob and Laura and Buddy and Sally.

Nowadays too there are please-sayers aplenty getting their share of goody-goody glory. Melissa Gilbert says please. And so does everyone else on the prairie. And everyone on Walton's Mountain, too. Dondi still says it with an Italian accent. The Osmonds say please to each other, even though they're related. Ditto the Partridge Family. Amy Carter actually tried to teach Uncle Billy to say it. (Of course, she failed. Billy will always be a Real Kid.)

And there are plenty of others who, despite honor roll and Emily Post, have managed to push (and shove and nag) their way into Real Kid prominence. Indeed, on Real Kid Old Timers' Day the conversation inevitably turns to a no-holds-barred debate over whether the Real Kids of yesterday could beat the Real Kids of today.

In numbers, at least, today's Real Kids are right up

there. The air waves are thick with them. Gary Coleman is a Real Kid. So is Linda Blair. And Emanuel Lewis. And Ricky Schroeder. And Elliot—even if he did let E.T. phone home.

Kristine, Kevin, Jodie, Jennifer, Lisa, and everyone else who Can't Do That on Television are Real Kids.

Craig Warnock is a Real Kid, as are all his fellow Time Bandits: Randy, Wally, Vermin, and all the rest of the size 6x tights-and-tunic crowd.

Fonzie is a Real Kid. So is Fozzie. And Kermit. And Miss Piggy.

"Sesame Street" is full of them. Grover, Cookie Monster, Oscar the Grouch, and even old buddy Burt are really Real Kids, and everyone knows Ernie is one.

No one knows if Brooke Shields is a Real Kid. Or cares.

There are plenty of big Real Kids around too. Baseball is loaded with them. Billy Martin is one, as he proves every time he opens his mouth, or kicks dirt, or both. Ditto Howard Cosell, mouth only. Pete Rose is a Real Kid—as is any 40-plus–year-old who thinks the only thing worth living for is baseball. Willie Mays is the kind of Real Kid who, if they don't let him play his way, just won't play at all.

Although most Real Kids don't play tennis, a few tennis stars are clearly Real Kids. Think about it the next time McEnroe plays Connors.

Eddie Murphy is a Real Kid. So are Dan Ackroyd and Gilda Radner and Steve Martin and Charlie Callas. And anyone else who spends the best part of the day making funny faces and disgusting noises.

Jim Bouton, Joe Bonanno, John Dean, and Woodward and Bernstein are all Real Kids. (Everyone knows Real Kids can't keep secrets.)

Yes, these are good times for Real Kids. And indeed, there is a glow on the Real Kid horizon. It seems there is every reason to expect—in light of his early performances before the camera, anyway—that Prince William himself may be one royal Real Kid. Just like his Uncle Andrew.

Other real kids past and present include:

ET
the Munchkins
Soupy Sales
Shirley Temple
Mickey Rooney
Andy Rooney
Ty Cobb
Tom Sawyer
Ronald McDonald
Ronald Reagan
Ricky Nelson
Ozzie Nelson
Oscar Madison
Howdy Doody
Princess Di
Little Lulu
Mick Jagger
Mrs. Thatcher
Dudley Moore
Billy the (Real) Kid
Mozart
Robin
and Jerry Lewis until he broke up with Dean Martin.

While the please-sayers count among their numbers:

Dinah Shore
Dr. Joyce Brothers
Bowie Kuhn
The Brady Bunch
Nancy Reagan
Ron, Jr.
Richard Nixon (Real kids don't carry attaché cases.)
David Nelson
Felix Unger (Real kids named Felix go by nick-
    names.)
Princess Anne
Queen Elizabeth
The entire King Family
Everybody who was ever in the New Christy Min-
    strels
Halston
Mr. Smith

Finally, there are those Real Kids who are Really Midgets:

Andy Hardy
Tatum O'Neal
Jerry Mahoney

6 GOLDEN MOMENTS IN REAL

4000 B.C.
The invention of the
wheel foreshadows the
skateboard.

c. 1816
The invention of the
bicycle solves the
problem of what to ask
for on your seventh,
eighth, ninth, tenth, and
eleventh birthdays.

346 BC
Ten-year-old Alexander
complains to his mother
that there's nothing to
do. Asks Aristotle where
Persia is.

1876
George Custer, Jr., tells
his father, "I'm staying
home."

1764
Mozart refuses to play
duets with his sister.

KID HISTORY

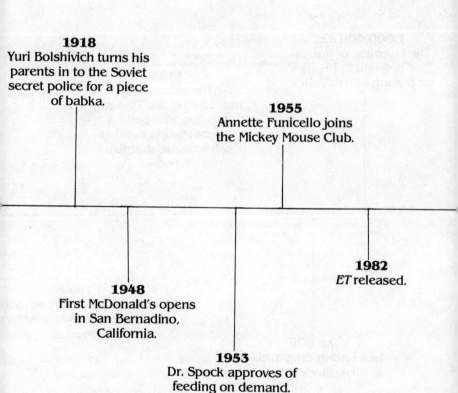

1918
Yuri Bolshivich turns his
parents in to the Soviet
secret police for a piece
of babka.

1955
Annette Funicello joins
the Mickey Mouse Club.

1982
ET released.

1948
First McDonald's opens
in San Bernadino,
California.

1953
Dr. Spock approves of
feeding on demand.

7 DARK MOMENTS IN REAL

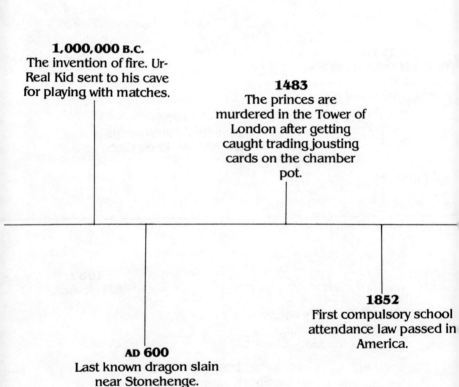

1,000,000 B.C.
The invention of fire. Ur-
Real Kid sent to his cave
for playing with matches.

1483
The princes are
murdered in the Tower of
London after getting
caught trading jousting
cards on the chamber
pot.

AD 600
Last known dragon slain
near Stonehenge.

1852
First compulsory school
attendance law passed in
America.

KID HISTORY

1876
The invention of the telephone enables teachers to call home.

1974
Sunny Jim orange drink goes off the market.

1945
Real Kids warned repeatedly to "just wait till your father comes home" finally find out what that means.

1984
Real Kids Don't Say Please published.

He's got to stop playing with fire, Org . . . that's
the second dinner he's ruined this week.

⑧ A GUIDE TO REAL KID ETHICS

Real Kids are nobody's fools.

Between the time he turns from tot to teen, a Real Kid possesses a clarity of vision enabling him to see through all the nonsense the adult world foists on children—till they come of age and start foisting themselves. No Real Kid ever bought land in Florida.

Real Kids know it's not really the thought that counts —especially when the gift is something you've got two of already. And they know that, "blessed" aside, it's still a whole lot better to receive than to give.

When the dust clears behind them, Real Kids are convinced it hurt them a whole lot more than it did you. In fact, they have their doubts about whether it hurt you at all.

Real Kids cheat. They know that when the equipment is packed up and the sodas passed around, someone may ask the final score, but nobody gives diddly about how you played the game.

Real Kids—especially those under 4´6"—just don't believe small is beautiful.

Real Kids have learned that, if at first you don't succeed, you should let your father do it.

Real Kids don't really understand what it means to "do unto others." And they're absolutely positive they don't want anybody doing unto them.

Real Kids figure it would save a lot of time if all the people who keep asking whether they "do that to the furniture at home" would just assume that they do.

Real Kids generally don't do as you say or as you do. They definitely do not "do as they're told."

Real Kids don't figure it's a good idea to "put off till tomorrow." Sometime next week is definitely soon enough for something you should've done today.

All this is not to say that there are no tried-and-true tenets dear to the Real Kid heart. Among the truths Real Kids would hold to be self-evident—if they knew what that meant—are:

"Nothing beats a Coke and pizza."

"Wednesday is Prince Spaghetti Day."

"You can tell it's Mattel; it's swell."

When it comes to seeing through a fake (i.e., a "phony baloney"), Real Kids' eyes are 20-20. Unlike adults, Real Kids know better than to take politicians seriously. (In fact, they know better than to listen to them at all.)

Real Kids take their parents seriously only for about a week before Christmas or their birthday.

Real Kids never take other kids seriously. Especially not if the others are Real Kids.

A Real Kid with a great screwball once said, "You gotta believe." Generally, though, Real Kids just don't buy it. Real Kids don't believe in Santa Claus, or the Tooth Fairy, or the Easter Bunny. (Though they let their parents go on thinking they do just as long as the loot keeps rolling in.)

They not only don't believe in fairies, they don't believe in Peter Pan, Wendy, or James Barrie.

They don't believe that anyone who makes them go to bed before "Dallas" can possibly be doing it for their own good.

Real Kids don't believe in talking frogs, flying nannies, Howard Hughes, or Mr. Rogers. Of course, Real Kids do believe in Superman; but they draw the line at Perry White.

Finally, a word about brotherhood. Unlike some of their parents, Real Kids are not prejudiced. They just don't like anyone who looks, acts, walks, talks, smiles, or dresses funny.

Real Kid
Surprise
Quiz #1

Q: Why did the Real Kid cross the road?

A: I didn't! I swear!

EQUATIONS

Taking your kid sister to the movies

Taking your kid sister to the movies and sitting with her till the end

Taking your kid sister to the movies and coming home without her

Taking milk of magnesia and/or an enema

Not telling your mother what you saw your older sister doing in her boyfriend's car

Not telling your father what you saw your older brother doing with his girl friend in his car

Not telling your mother what you saw your father doing to your older brother's girl friend in *his* car

Getting an A in math

Getting an A in math—Getting an F in reading

Losing your key

Losing your watch

Eating spinach

Not eating spinach

One buttered popcorn + One large Coke

One buttered popcorn + One large Coke + Getting to
   stay up for "Dallas" on two consecutive Fridays

Two buttered popcorns + Two large Cokes + A lot of
   weekends home

One coloring book, water pistol, or digital watch,
   depending on age

One application of eyeshadow, mascara, and lip gloss
   or One semi-annual room cleaning, depending on
   sex

Free use of his baseball mitt, stereo, or after shave for
   a week

Chow mein, pizza, or Kentucky Fried Chicken on
   demand for life or until the divorce, whichever
   comes first

One full day at the amusement park of your choice

One full day at the library of your choice

One new key + One long lecture

One long lecture

Seconds on dessert

Seconds on spinach

10

THE REAL KIDS'
PHYSICAL
FITNESS
PROGRAM

A lot of manufacturers these days think there's money to be made in outfitting junior Bruce Jenners and Chrissie Everts. And they may sell their share of size-two Nikes. They're likely to be stuck, however, with racks of mother-daughter and father-son warm-up suits.

Real Kids have their own methods of staying in shape. To wit:

Real Kids don't jog. They don't do calisthenics. They think isometrics comes between geometry and algebra. And they still think the *Nautilus* belongs to Captain Nemo.

Real Kids don't warm up.

Real Kids don't time anything except how long they can hold their breath under water.

Real Kids don't do yoga. They don't meditate. They think that people who do are weird.

Real Kids don't count calories. They think eating a lot makes you healthy.

Finally, Real Kids never listen to reports by the American Council on Youth Fitness. They're too busy playing outside.

She said they *are* on their best behavior.

11

REAL FOOD

Real Kids don't eat health foods. (They don't think of anything in the vitamin aisle as food.)

Real Kids, of course, don't eat quiche—or sushi or guacamole or hors d'oeuvres. They don't eat anything that's spelled funny. Real Kids don't eat acorn squash. Or summer squash, or butternut squash, or zucchini. They not only don't eat spinach, they don't eat broccoli or brussels sprouts or kale. In fact, most Real Kids won't eat *anything* green. Real Kids eat only white lettuce, with or without bottled dressing.

Real Kids reject eggplant, no matter how it's disguised. They will eat corn on the cob, but prefer Del Monte Niblets. Real Kids think that carrots come in cubes. No self-respecting Real Kid eats the lima beans in mixed vegetables.

Real Kids don't know the names of French cheeses. They are the *only* people who like Velveeta. They like it because it doesn't taste like cheese. Real Kids like to squeeze Cheez-Wiz onto crackers, but they don't necessarily eat the crackers.

Real Kids don't eat oatmeal for breakfast—or Wheatena or farina. They absolutely will not eat wheat germ. In general, Real Kids don't eat any "cereals" that look like turtle food. Real Kids like cereals in which sugar is listed as the first ingredient and honey or glucose as the second or third.

For lunch, Real Kids like Wonder Bread best. In fact, they may not put their peanut butter and jelly on anything else. Real Kids do not eat whole wheat bread. Or any bread with "things" in it. Real Kids leave the crusts.

Real Kids like cold cuts for lunch. They use lots of ketchup. They use mustard, too, but not if it's brown. Real Kids don't think that real hamburgers can be made at home.

Real Kids don't eat fish. They eat tuna only because they know it isn't really fish. Real Kids will not eat *anything* if a whole fish is placed on the table: it is a bad omen if your food looks back at you.

Real Kids go through periods in which they eat *only* between meals.

Real Kids eat Oreos in layers. They scrape the chocolate off Chocograhams with their teeth and peel it off Mallomars with their fingernails. However, Real Kids do not dismember—or otherwise handle—Fig Newtons; Fig Newtons just don't look like cookies—or like anything else edible.

Real Kids think dates are figs. They don't eat either.

Real Kids know the difference between ice cream and frozen yogurt. And between ice cream and ice milk. On a make-your-own sundae, they try to use chocolate, marshmallow, *and* butterscotch topping. Real Kids don't care for sherbet.

Real Kids don't think the cones their mothers fill at home are ice cream cones. When given a choice, they go for parlor flavors with candy or cookie names. Real Kids are not wild about Neapolitan ice cream. If their mother buys it anyway, they scoop out the chocolate and vanilla and leave the strawberry in an untouched frozen column. If she insists on serving it all in a dish, a Real Kid will stir it into a liquid the color of calamine lotion and slurp it off the spoon like soup.

Real Kids don't eat the peanuts in Cracker Jacks. And they think the prizes are dumb.

Real Kids know that Reggie is still just a home-run hitter. They look for a candy bar that offers good value—a good *eating* candy bar. A Real Kid knows this doesn't necessarily mean a big candy bar: a moderate-sized frozen Milky Way or a Turkish Taffy takes longer to eat than, say, a large box of Junior Mints. The chew-factor must be taken into account, as well as the time-extension offered by the need to unglue one's teeth.

Real Kids will not buy Charleston Chews. And they wonder who does.

M & M's melt in Real Kids' hands.

To their parents' continuing horror, Real Kids still crave red hots, candy corn (seasonal craving; appears only in October), and those little orange things shaped like peanuts.

Real Kids know Granola bars aren't candy.

Real Kids' favorite flavor is not chocolate or vanilla—it is red. In general, any food that turns your tongue red can be considered a Real Kids' food.

Similarly, a drink that leaves a chocolate mustache is a Real Kids' drink. A McDonald's thick shake is a great Real Kids' drink, as is any drink you're better off eating with a spoon.

Postum is not a Real Kids' drink. Neither is hot tea, especially not those funny-smelling herb teas. In fact, Real Kids won't drink anything hot unless they're sick. Except for cocoa (which leaves a chocolate mustache).

Real Kids don't drink Perrier. They still like Kool-Aid, despite Jim Jones.

Real Kids like juices that stain—except for prune juice, which Real Kids suspect isn't a juice. Real Kids don't like thick juices that come in jars and have to be mixed with water, like papaya juice. They do, however, like "juices" made from granules (e.g., Tang, or better yet, Wyler's Fruit Punch). Real Kids prefer Tropicana or Minute Maid to fresh-squeezed: juice shouldn't have gook in it.

Real Kids don't drink skim milk. Many don't drink milk at all unless it has been mixed with equal parts of Hershey's Syrup. Adding ice cream and seltzer can't hurt, either. Real Kids can drink Hershey's straight from the can.

Real Kids don't drink diet soda.

Although Real Kids hate beer and wine, they may not admit it if a real adult gives them a taste.

Real Kids have their own unique sense of nutritional balance. Thus, they serve themselves more saltines than chicken soup, stuffing than turkey, syrup than pancakes, and more Reddi-Whip than strawberries and shortcake combined.

And Real Kids have their own food etiquette. Real Kids don't tuck their napkins under their chin or spread them on their lap either. They use them to hide vegetables in (provided there is no uneaten potato skin on hand to serve that purpose). Real Kids hold their forks like shovels—often in the hand opposite the one they're eating with.

Real Kids don't clean their plates no matter how often they hear about the starving people in China. They never finish their cereal. (Hours later, when it has turned to a beige semi-liquid, their mothers finish it for them.)

Real Kids do play with their food, talk with their mouths full, and swallow without chewing.

Real Kids don't say grace.

Anyone who has ever eaten out with a Real Kid knows what an adventure it can be. The moment you arrive, you are transported at breathtaking speed into the darkest reaches of the restaurant as maitre d', waiters, and busboys glower at you with fierce suspicion. Even while still on the way to the table, a Real Kid may have managed to knock over a tray of pitchers, or at least a place setting or two, and to poke six or eight diners with his elbows.

If the table has not yet been cleared from previous diners, Real Kids are in Real Kids' heaven. They examine plates of leftovers under crushed cigarette butts, probe the nature of half-eaten desserts, and count the uncollected tip.

If there is already water on the table, a Real Kid will spill it. If there isn't, he will ask for some—which he'll spill as soon as it comes. (Real Kids never drink water at home, but miss it sorely when it is not served at a restaurant.)

Real Kids want their own menu and somehow manage to cover it with foody fingerprints even before any food has arrived. Ordering gives Real Kids a chance to show off imagination at its apex. If they are dining at a Chinese restaurant, they will probably ask for a hamburger. At a fish house, they're dying for spaghetti and meatballs.

Whatever they order, Real Kids will always ask for a Coke; they've found through experience that things

That must be the little inconvenience one can expect at a family style restaurant.

really do go better with it. Real Kids never order tomato juice as an appetizer. They will ask the waiter to describe every dessert on the menu.

After the order has been taken, Real Kids will ask up to two times per minute: "When is it gonna get here?" While waiting, Real Kids like to fill in the blank spaces on their placemats—or whatever else (napkins, wine list, tablecloth) comes readily to hand.

By the time the food arrives, Real Kids may have emptied the bread basket and their and everybody else's butter dishes. This likely contributes to the Real Kids' sudden loss of appetite upon being served. (This loss of appetite is temporary; Real Kids unfailingly make room for at least one dessert.) Regardless of how much or how little they eat, Real Kids leave the messiest place.

Real Kids will probably ask to be excused at least twice to go to the rest room. Having gone, they may remain absent for up to twenty minutes at a time. A search will sometimes turn them up lurking around—or under—another family's table.

Unfortunately, whether or not you look for *them*, Real Kids will find *you* by the time the waiter brings the check, thus making it impossible for you to slip to the door pretending you don't know them.

Given all the above, it is wise to choose carefully where you dare to dine with Real Kids, bearing in mind their own not negligible preferences:

1. Real Kids like restaurants that prominently advertise how many billions of something have been served.

2. Real Kids don't like any restaurant where a hamburger is called a Salisbury steak.

3. Real Kids are uncomfortable in any restaurant lit by candlelight—except Pizza Hut.

4. Real Kids don't like restaurants where there is soft music. At the kind of restaurant Real Kids like, the music is loud but you can hardly hear it over the screaming.

5. Real Kids can't wait to get at a salad bar. Even though they will spit out three-quarters of their selections.

6. Real Kids like any restaurant you can drive through.

7. Real Kids prefer restaurants with pictures of club sandwiches and banana splits on the menu.

8. Real Kids like restaurants that serve on map-of-Delaware or what's-wrong-in-this-picture placemats.

9. Real Kids go for restaurants that have mile-high desserts in Art Deco display windows.

10. Real Kids will ask to be taken back to restaurants that keep multicolored mints next to the cash register.

Finally, it is wise to resist when Real Kids beg you to take them to all-you-can-eat restaurants. In the car, their enthusiasm seems as unbounded as a bottomless orange soda. But as soon as a Real Kid gets to the table, he orders water, empties the bread basket and all the butter in the butter dishes, and loses his appetite. Until the waiter mentions dessert—which is, of course, not included.

12 FOUR THINGS REAL KIDS CHEW

1. Life Savers

2. Pencils (including eraser tips)

3. Fingernails

4. Toenails

13 SCHOOL DAYS: BEYOND THE 3 R'S

Perhaps no other setting brings out the qualities that distinguish Real Kids from please-sayers more than school. Here a make-it-or-break-it challenge confronts the would-be Real Kid. For here, manna is showered on those who say please. Here, words of praise, giddy percents in the upper-nineties, and row on row of gum-backed gold stars are bestowed upon those neatly dressed, pressed, and folded correct-answermongers known as teachers' pets, who sit at desks with hands folded, bring in autumn leaf collections or pictures of things-made-out-of-cotton as instructed, and tell on the Real Kids for trading bubble-gum cards in the bathroom.

Real Kids will not compromise their integrity for all the pedagogic and parental approbation this might buy. They would rather write, "I will not spit in the cafeteria" a thousand times than not spit in the cafeteria once.

There is, however, some practicality in the decision to remain a Real Kid even at the expense of PTA approval. On the way home from school—in that twilight area known vaguely as "out of school bounds"—Real Kids regularly beat teachers' pets to a pulp.*

---

*Actually, there are three and not two categories of schoolchildren: Real Kids, teachers' pets, and losers. Here, we will worry only about the Real Kids and the teachers' pets, and just forget about the losers. Like everyone else does.

We've spent a lot of hard earned money on your back-to-school wardrobe. The least you can do is look it!

Every Real Kid knows that to maintain his standing, he must follow these time-honored rules:

Real Kids get to school on their own steam. If Mom insists on driving, they insist on getting dropped off a block away.

When Real Kids see their teacher driving to school, they pretend not to look, and then tell the other kids they saw her smoking or making out with somebody.

Real Kids don't dress up on the first day of school. They try not to get up on the morning of the second.

Real Kids don't rush to the store the first week of September to buy back-to-school supplies. When they do get around to their shopping, Real Kids don't choose weights-and-measurements book covers. They do up their books in covers with pictures of John Travolta and Olivia Newton-John. In the course of the semester they draw in the private parts.

Real Kids crave Smurf pencil cases with "eyes." Over their mothers' objections, they demand big green disk erasers with bristles. Though a seeming frivolity, these roll into action by the second or third week of the term, after Real Kids have bitten off the eraser-tips from all their pencils. (Three days out of five, real kids don't have a pencil anyway. When they borrow one—from one of those ever-ready A-students with a pencil case stuffed with writing implements sharpened to lethal perfection —they give it back with the point broken, the eraser bitten off, and maybe a few tooth marks in between.)

Real Kids prefer pens to pencils for writing on desks. They know that only a quality ballpoint cuts deeply enough into desk-veneer to make an impression that will put a hole into any page written over it from then on.

Real Kids don't raise their hand if they can't see the blackboard. They don't volunteer. They don't do extra credit. They don't win spelling bees. They don't even try. (On a hot day, a Real Kid can be out of the contest on a word like "chair.")

Occasionally, a Real Kid may get honorable mention for a fire-prevention essay or a dental limerick, but it generally turns out that his father "gave him the idea."

Real Kids get help on their science projects but sometimes don't bother to bring them in.

Real Kids forget their tie on assembly day. Then they lose the one their teacher lent them. They wear sneakers to school whenever they can get out of the house in them, but leave them home when they have gym.

A Real Kid is mortified if his teacher reads his A-composition to the class or tells some chronic behavior problem to behave more like *he* does. To a Real Kid, a U in conduct is the greatest badge of honor he can brandish among his friends. With a U in conduct, a Real Kid need not apologize for an A- in social studies.

A Real Kid puts real heart into his excuses for late and missing work. Dogs, baby sisters, grandmothers, and garbage disposals all figure prominently in his excuses, sometimes all in the same story. The real joy in this comes when a Real Kid gets his teacher to address to him statements beginning with: "If you could apply as much effort to math as to thinking up excuses . . ."

And Real Kids really know how to work over a substitute teacher. On a good day, a classful of Real Kids can arrange it so that after terrorizing a sub from 9 to 3, the principal keeps the *sub* after class for a reprimand.

Real Kids know how to make the most out of school trips. On such trips, a Real Kid can make the class-mother sweat at a hundred paces. Especially if he's her Real Kid.

Lunch is, of course, the natural apex of a Real Kid's school day. And no Real Kid is unaware of the rules that reign in this golden hour. Whether they carry lunch (in a bag or coat pocket, never in a Flintstones lunchbox) or buy it, Real Kids are without the means to eat at least once a week. When they do remember to bring their lunch, they try to trade their sandwich for Ring Dings. Or their Ring Dings for Twinkies. When they have lunch money, they spend as little as they can and then shoot the rest on Devil Dogs on the way home.

Every phase of school life is governed by such etiquette, and Real Kids with an instinct for survival know
that they must observe it. Thus, Real Kids know it isn't
good form to:

a) get excited about high marks,
b) look forward to getting report cards,
c) cry when sent to the principal's office,
d) do the exercises in gym,
e) return promptly from the bathroom,
f) raise their hand more than twice a day,
g) sing at assembly,
h) read their compositions in class,
i) volunteer for the color guard.

In short, a true Real Kid claims to be dying to graduate
and get the #%*#&! out of school but does whatever he
can not to.

"Oops" is not considered an apology, young man.

The Real Kids'
Ideal School Day

8:55 Arrive in yard to learn teacher involved in car accident.

8:56 Rumor started that teacher was on her way to an abortion clinic.

9:30 Principal realizes class still out in yard; sends yard monitor to round it up.

10:30 Assistant principal rounds up class and yard-monitor.

10:35 Assistant principal chooses class clown to watch class until substitute arrives.

11:05 Substitute arrives and tells class clown to get off her desk. Starts taking attendance.

11:55 Attendance finished. Class dismissed early for lunch.

1:15 Students return from lunch and tell substitute class has gym at 1:00.

1:45 Substitute finds gymnasium.

1:46 Substitute informed by gym teacher that class does not have gym that period.

1:47 Class provokes argument between gym teacher and substitute.

2:10 Substitute finds way back to classroom.

2:11 Class tells substitute Tuesday is "Game Day."

2:35 Substitute realizes it is Wednesday.

2:45 Class dismissed after convincing substitute that clock is fifteen minutes slow.

Real Kid
Surprise
Quiz #2

Q: How many Real Kids does it take to change a light bulb?

A: But I didn't break it!

14

THE REAL KIDS' CALENDAR

September

Su	M	T	W	Th	F	Sa
	1	2	3	4	5	6
7 Last day of summer.	8 school begins.	9 295 days till school ends.	10	11 Easy days.	12	13 almost a Friday the 13ᵗʰ
14	15	16	17	18	19	20
21	22	23	24	25	26	27
28	29	30				

Possible sick days.

→

→

October

Su	M	T	W	Th	F	Sa
			1	2	3	4
5	6	7	8	9	10	11
12	13	14	15	16	17	18
19	20	21	22	23	24	25
26	27	28	29	30	31	

More possible

sick days →

→

The week before Halloween. (Remind Mom to buy candy.)

HALLOWEEN!

54 / *Real Kids Don't Say Please*

November

Su	M	T	W	Th	F	Sa
						1
2	3	4	5	6	7	8
9	10	11	12	13	14	15
16	17	18	19	20	21	22
23	24	25	26	27	28	29
30						

The week after Halloween.
(Remind Mom to buy candy.)

A good time to sprain

something.

Thanks-giving   Beginning of Christmas season.

December

Su	M	T	W	Th	F	Sa
	1	2	3	4	5	6
7	8	9	10	11	12	13
14	15	16	17	18	19	20
21	22	23	24	25	26	27
28	29	30	31			

CHRISTMAS!

January

Su	M	T	W	Th	F	Sa
				1	2	3
				still really Christmas		
4	5	6	7	8	9	10
	Possible snow days →					
11	12	13	14	15	16	17
18	19	20	21	22	23	24
25	26	27	28	29	30	31

February

Su	M	T	W	Th	F	Sa
1	2	3	4	5	6	7
						official
8	9	10	11	12	13	14
long weekend.						official
15	16	17	18	19	20	21
long weekend.						Unoffical
22	23	24	25	26	27	28
long weekend?						

March

Su	M	T	W	Th	F	Sa
1	2	3	4	5	6	7
8	9	10	11	12	13	14
15	16	17	18	19	20	21
22	23	24	25	26	27	28
29	30	31				

Possible month for Easter vacation.

April

Su	M	T	W	Th	F	Sa
		1			3	4
5	6	7	8	9	10	11
12	13	14	15	16	17	18
19	20	21	22	23	24	25
26	27	28	29	30		

Another possible month for Easter vacation.

May

Su	M	T	W	Th	F	Sa
					1	2
3	4	5	6	7	8	9
10	11	12	13	14	15	16
17	18	19	20	21	22	23
24	25	26	27	28	29	30
31						

Very Long Month.

June

Su	M	T	W	Th	F	Sa
	1	2	3	4	5	6
7	8	9	10	11	12	13
14	15	16	17	18	19	20
21	22	23	24	25	26	27
28	29	30				

The month before Summer.

July

Su	M	T	W	Th	F	Sa
			1	2	3	4
5	6	7	8	9	10	11
12	13	14	15	16	17	18
19	20	21	22	23	24	25
26	27	28	29	30	31	

August

Su	M	T	W	Th	F	Sa
						1
2	3	4	5	6	7	8
9	10	11	12	13	14	15
16	17	18	19	20	21	22
23	24	25	26	27	28	29
30	31					

SUMMER!

15 WHAT THE WELL-DRESSED REAL KID WILL (AND WON'T) WEAR

Although Real Kids don't like shopping for clothes or receiving them as presents, they are not unparticular about what they wear. Real Kids like to have a hand in choosing the day's garb and may prove surprisingly resistant to suggestions that a flowered skirt doesn't really go with a striped leotard or that the vest would look better over a shirt.

Given the opportunity, Real Kids will wear certain favored items long past raghood (a Real Kid is loyal to the clothes he likes), while leaving others to be outgrown and turned over to the Salvation Army, tags intact.

Among the items that will stay permanently clean and folded in a Real Kid's drawer or closet are:

Bermuda shorts
designer jeans
alligator shirts
alligator slacks
alligator socks
dickies
cardigans
anything with their initials
anything in a color they don't know the name of
anything that itches
hats

Age is not a criterion by which Real Kids determine their wardrobe preferences: They hate both new shoes and old hand-me-downs. Price, on the other hand, is: No Real Kid wants to wear something so expensive that his mother will ask where it is when he loses it.

What, then, does the Real Kid like to wear?

Underwear with holes
Wranglers
Sneakers
and an E.T. tee-shirt
                                        All the time.

Oh, thank you, mother Richards. It's just what he
wanted.

16 GIFTS TO GIVE THE REAL KID WHO HAS EVERYTHING

Nowadays most Real Kids fit into this category. But since it is an axiom that to no Real Kid is everything ever enough, herein is a list of Real Kid gift do's and don'ts:

Gifts Real Kids Don't Appreciate

1) savings bonds
2) pen-and-pencil sets
3) books with a lot of print
4) books without a lot of print
5) educational vehicles thinly disguised as toys
6) games they already have
7) anything made by an aunt
8) underwear

In addition to #8 above, Real Kids don't appreciate gifts of clothing in general. And they downright resent getting clothes that don't fit. In fact, one method Real Kids use to sabotage clothing gifts is to stand funny when they try them on so they look like they don't fit. (Other methods include snagging them on the gift box, ripping off tags with their teeth, and wearing them to play in the rain—and falling down.)

There are, of course, a few clothing items Real Kids do appreciate receiving (soccer shirts, shirts with swamp animals dressed for poolside with jiggling "eyes" sent north by grandmothers in Miami, cowboy boots, cowboy belts, Superhero Underoos, and anything with a college name or a Smurf on it.) Naturally, these might be added to the items directly following:

Gifts Real Kids Do Appreciate

1) any toy advertised on television at least six times a day
2) any toy their brother or sister gets (these are "needs")
3) any toy the other kids on the block have
4) any toy the other kids on the block don't have
5) anything electronic
6) anything they wouldn't be allowed to have if it weren't a gift
7) gifts they can eat (especially those that conform to item #6 above)
8) hard cash

Although they like toys, Real Kids appreciate even more getting real stuff (tools, arts and crafts supplies, sporting goods, knives, guns). And the real stuff Real Kids really appreciate is that which can be included among the items in the last category:

Gifts Real Kids Appreciate But Their Parents Don't

1) a dog (or anything you have to feed)
2) modeling clay
3) anything that flies
4) toys with batteries not included
5) toys with "simple" assembly required
6) ant farms
7) drums
8) pastels

Oh yes, there are two details relevant to Real Kid gift presentation:

1) Real Kids don't read cards.
2) If it isn't wrapped, it isn't a present. You still owe them.

17

GETTING THERE

For Real Kids, this is *more* than half the fun, regardless either of destination or vehicle used to reach it. In fact, the only form of transit Real Kids don't officially recognize is walking: if God had intended human beings to walk, He wouldn't have created drive-ins.

Of course, as everybody, Real Kids have their preferences among means of transportation, some of which defy convention. For example, Real Kids are the only people who would rather take the bus. This is because buses are the ideal setting for singing "100 Bottles of Beer." On bus rides of an hour or more, Real Kids will sing every verse of "100 Bottles of Beer." Twice.

Of course, trains also offer undeniable opportunities. On trains, Real Kids can walk through all the cars bothering the other passengers. (On planes, they don't have to; they can bother everyone right from their own seat.)

But buses, though less spacious, provide one pastime that makes bothering the other passengers seem a waste of time: Bothering the driver. Standing in the aisle, making faces in his mirror, or dropping articles of clothing out the window are only a few among the infinite means by which the Real Kid can achieve this goal. And a victory is scored every time the driver glowers or maybe even hollers at your reflection in his rearview mirror, or, better still, stops the bus and threatens to throw you off "if he catches you doing that again."

To facilitate these endeavors, Real Kids generally try to sit in the back of the bus—in that gray area of five-seats-across where a driver may have to search repeatedly to locate the precise source of "that disgusting noise" or the face and body attached to the leg that's been sticking out of the window for the last six miles.

If all the seats in the back are occupied, Real Kids know next best is the one behind the driver's seat. Here, a Real Kid with finesse can grill a novice operator for the duration of the journey to find out where he lives, how many miles he drives a day, whether he keeps a toothbrush on the bus, and are we there yet, are we there yet, are we there yet. (Of course, on uncrowded buses, Real Kids will intermittently occupy seats both front and rear—and several in between—in the course of a journey.)

Seating is equally important on car trips, long or short. On short rides, Real Kids vie for the privilege of sitting next to their parents (even though at home they do everything in their power to avoid them). However, if this means sitting up front next to a sister or brother, Real Kids will opt for the rear. There is one paramount rule: Real Siblings don't sit next to each other if they can help it. Even if it means staying home.

On long car trips, Real Kids always prefer the back seat. The back seat is the best place for doing "special effects." Real Kids are particularly keen on riding in the back of station wagons because they get to make faces at the drivers who come up behind their parents' car. (Parents whose Real Kids ride in the back of the station wagon might think twice before flashing their brights at the truckdriver who cut them off "for no good reason.") Also, station wagons and vans provide buffer zones when parents reach back to separate two Real Kids locked in a death grip or to haul in the child threatened with being dropped onto the highway if he doesn't "let me play with it."

Whatever seat they are assigned, however, Real Kids will spend as much time as possible standing. They will sit only when forced to wear their seat belts, and then will make sure everyone else is wearing his by giving all the belts a gentle TUG. On long car trips this unofficial inspection may be repeated once every fifteen minutes or every ten miles, whichever comes first.

Real Kids love long car trips mainly because long car trips mean long-car-trip food. Given the chance, a Real Kid will eat all the food packed for a two-day trip in the first hour and a half. Then he will say he's hungry every time he sees a McDonald's or HoJo's billboard. For some reason Real Kids also beg to eat at places like Stuckey's. If a parent is foolish enough to indulge him, a Real Kid will then beg to be bought a souvenir, which he will break or lose shortly before approaching the next Stuckey's. Some parents try to avoid this cycle by buying a peanut-log or salt water taffy. But a Real Kid will polish this off before leaving the restaurant and then beg for a souvenir.

When asked, Real Kids never have to use the facilities at a rest stop their parents have pulled into. Instead, they get the urge to go within seconds after the car has pulled back onto the highway.

To get a few moments of peace, parents of Real Kids often encourage them to nap for part of the ride. Toward this end, they pack blankets and pillows and even sit with all the luggage piled in the front seat to provide room for the kids to stretch out in back. Regardless of all these efforts, Real Kids generally won't nap during car rides. If they nap at all, they fall asleep about five minutes before the end of the trip.

A corollary traveling rule is that Real Kids don't sleep on overnight flights. And they don't seem to feel that other passengers ought to. To occupy the hours, Real Kids zealously leaf through all the issues of *Time, Tennis,* and *Popular Mechanics* they managed to scoop up as they boarded, open up their barf bag, open up your barf bag, and check up on what the stewardesses and the people in First Class are doing.

In flight, Real Kids keep busier than the pilot. Real Kids are the only people who read the emergency exit cards—out loud. They see how fast they can get out of their seat belts. They look for their life preserver. They open and shut the window shade. They see whether their light goes on. And off. And on. And off. And on. And they see whether the other lights in their row go on. And off. And on. They adjust their seat to full recline, then snap it bolt upright, then work incessantly on that perfect adjustment of its angle that always seems just one more adjustment away.

And then there is the rest room. Real Kids are never more incontinent than on an airplane, especially when they have to squeeze from a window seat into an aisle momentarily clogged by a beverage cart and two stewardesses pouring hot coffee. They usually have to go worst when the door marker seems permanently stuck on *Occupied* and the waiting line is stretching halfway up the smoking section.

A trip to the restroom is a journey in itself. On entering, Real Kids shift the *Occupied-Vacant* lever back and forth several times to test if the door really locks. After watching the blue water in the toilet swirl down four or five flushes-worth, they find a use for all the other facilities: unwrap a new soap or two, run the hot and cold water, help themselves to a few tissues, stick something into the electric shaver socket, and stuff a wad of paper towels down the shoot that says "no paper please" to see what will happen.

Real Kids generally time their trips to the rest room so as to get back to their seats shortly after the meal trays have been set down. And they will time their return trip to the rest room to fall shortly before the trays are picked up. (Really inventive Real Kids may squeeze in a separate trip for brushing their teeth—even when at home their mouths seem to have been set aside as a culture plate for pyorrhea.)

Consuming their meal along their usual guidelines for restaurant etiquette (see Real Food), Real Kids always store a little something—an open package of ketchup, half a piece of cheesecake, and opened-but-untouched carton of milk—in their magazine pouch for later, emergency consumption. And it is in this way that they make their most enduring impression on fellow travellers, as the morsel is generally still on hand for the perusal of the next passenger who occupies the seat.

All in all, it is perhaps no surprise that Real Kids know not to take it seriously when the flight attendant tells them to "come back and see us."

Of course I was young once, too. . . . It was right
before he came aboard!

18

HOW I SPENT MY SUMMER VACATION

On the Beach

All parents know that Real Kids love the beach. Most parents know that their children should be exposed to the sun gradually and should wait at least an hour after eating to go into the water. Here, however, are a few less-quoted items of beach lore of which no parent should be ignorant:

Real Kids don't wear Coppertone. Or Sea & Ski. Or Presun. They will not wear anything that makes their nose white. Real Kids don't keep their shoulders covered. They lose beach hats. On purpose.

Actually, Real Kids like getting sunburned because they enjoy peeling off blistered skin.

No matter how bright the sun, Real Kids don't wear sunglasses at the beach. (They are, however, more than willing to try them on by the gross in drugstores or at each others' houses.)

Real Kids squint a lot. And they complain that the sun is in their eyes.

They also complain that the sand is in their eyes. And their bathing suit. And their food.

And that they got salt water in their mouth. And their eyes. And their food.

Real Kids eat more at the beach than anywhere. And *ask* for more. It is axiomatic that the thermos will run out before a Real Kid's thirst.

Real Kids always go in the water right after eating. And they always *go* in the water right after eating. Real Kids never go in only up to their ankles. Unless they haven't taken off their shoes and socks yet.

Of course, Real Kids splash. And they like it when their lips turn blue.

Despite what most adults think, Real Kids actually enjoy playing Marco Polo. Driving everyone within twenty yards of the water crazy is only an added plus. Marco! . . . Polo! . . . Marco! . . . Polo!

There is strong evidence to suggest that, when in water, Real Kids really cannot hear the lifeguard's whistle or their mother's voice.

Real Kids usually walk on the rocks without their sandals. If they wear sandals at all (for example, when walking in the water), they wear somebody else's.

When Real Kids throw something around on the beach, they demonstrate an uncanny ability to hit old ladies. Generally front and back. When they're not throwing something around, they like spying on their older brother and his girl friend. Or on their older sister and the lifeguard.

Fortunately, some Real Kids actually enjoy building sand castles. Because most are crazy about knocking them down.

Here are a few other things Real Kids do at the beach:

chase things
bury things
find things
lose things
cut their feet
get splinters
get bitten
get bored

At Camp

A good counselor

—smokes
—hangs out with the other counselors
—lets you use her make-up or his after-shave
—has a picture of Olivia Newton-John and/or Elton
   John in his/her locker
—knows a few dirty songs
—knows lots of dirty words
—doesn't ask you why you weren't at archery
—will cheat to win the color war

19 THE ADVANTAGES AND DISADVANTAGES OF VISITING THE GRAND CANYON

The Advantages

1. You find out what a canyon is.

2. You get to tell your friends how great the Grand Canyon is.

3. You get to carry a knapsack.

4. You don't have to wear pajamas.

5. There's no place to wash your hands.

6. You get to eat a lot of hot dogs and hamburgers.

The Disadvantages

1. You can't keep nagging your parents about taking you to visit the Grand Canyon.

2. The Grand Canyon is boring.

3. You have to carry a knapsack.

4. You have to talk to your parents for eight days.

5. Your parents talk to you for eight days.

6. Gorp.

Awe-inspiring beauty doesn't *have* to *do* anything, son.

20   THE REAL KIDS' OSCARS

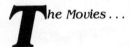

The Movies...

The Real Kids' top movies of all time are:

1) *E.T.*
2) *Raiders of the Lost Ark*
3) *Star Wars*
4) *The Empire Strikes Back*
5) *Return of the Jedi*
6) *Superman I*
7) *Superman II*
8) *Superman III*
9) *Close Encounters of the Third Kind*
10) *The Wizard of Oz*

and any and all sequels to the above.

It is worth nothing that, since the NBC peacock first spread its tail, Real Kids have become increasingly averse to black-and-white movies. A few films have escaped this general condemnation by airing on independent television networks at holiday time, sand-

wiched between Three Stooges and Abbott and Costello reruns—and masquerading as long, old TV programs. Thus, among Real Kids' favorite flicks—even
without popcorn and dollar-boxes of Milk Duds—must
be counted such minor epics as the *March of the
Wooden Soldiers, Heidi, Wee Willie Winkie,* and the Marx
Brothers comedies (although when dragged by their
parents to view these last in retrospective film houses,
Real Kids may find even slapstick boring).

Most black-and-white films, however, are reviled by
Real Kids, which is one reason why no black-and-white
foreign film can be counted among their favorites. (Of
course, Real Kids also hate color foreign films.)

Among the movies Real Kids give a "thumbs down" to
are:

State of Siege
Emanuelle
Darling
all movies based on plays
all movies starring Astaire and Rogers (or Astaire
    and anybody for that matter)
movies that feature Cary Grant wearing a tuxedo
movies that feature Marlene Dietrich wearing a
    tuxedo
all the parts of *Nicholas Nickleby*
any part of *Napoleon*
shorts (if it's not worth watching for an hour and a
    half, it's not worth watching)

And the Stars . . .

The Real Kids' top 10 male stars are:

1) E. T.
2) The guy in *Raiders of the Lost Ark*
3) Christopher Reeve
4) Harpo Marx
5) Groucho Marx
6) R2D2
7) The guy who played Luke Skywalker
8) Johnny Weissmuller
9) Cheetah
10) Jerry Lewis

And the female stars:

1) Judy Garland
2) Shirley Temple
3) Elliot's sister
4) Elliot's mother
5) Everybody who ever played Lois Lane
6) Everybody who ever played Jane
7) The Wicked Witch of the West/East (although they weren't sure she *was* a woman till she started serving Maxwell House)
8) Lucy
9) Laverne
10) Princess Leia

21 GREAL MOMENTS IN REAL KID CINEMA

"Pay no attention to that man behind the screen."
—The Wizard to Dorothy in *The Wizard of Oz*

"Phone home."

—E.T.

22

TV OR NOT TV: A REAL KIDS' TV GUIDE

*I*t's true: Real Kids watch too much TV. They know it. Everyone knows it. But what really gets them is when there's nothing on they want to watch. It's a real pain when the best choice is between "Merv Griffin," "Hour Magazine," and a PBS special on "The Making of Gandhi."

The hard fact is, when it comes to the tube, Real Kids will watch anything. True, they are bored practically to catatonia by network news, talky talk shows, and "Masterpiece Theatre." But they aren't about to get caught turning off the set. No way. If it comes to that, better to just leave the room or wait it out till the guy comes on at 10:00, asks parents if they know where their children are, and reminds them that they're still there watching.

As a result, Real Kids have become inveterate dial turners and, since the advent of cable, avid button pushers. In fact, Real Kids with cable spend more time changing the channels than watching any one in particular.

Cable Channel selector buttons have thus reconciled the old dilemma of what you watch when "Gilligan's Island" and "Love Boat" are on at the same time: Both, of course, and maybe a "Dobie Gillis" rerun on the side.

And cable and other innovations have done their share to fill up the vast wasteland with enough "great programs" to flesh out the seven-hour-a-day minimum viewing time (MVT) of your average Real Kid. The VCR has enabled the privileged Real Kid to store up enough action-packed hours in prime time to last through the famine of a Sunday morning or a Saturday afternoon. Indeed, with the likes of *Star Wars* and *Time Bandits* finally finding their way through HBO to their own private video libraries, Real Kids may never have to sit through a Ronald Reagan press conference again or flip back and forth between the PTL and 700 Clubs waiting for something funny to happen.

And if he's ever caught short—say, faced with newsmen on channels one through eighty-three all waiting for the Vice President to show up at the Zaire airport and talking motorcade routes with some guy with a heavy accent—the Real Kid always has one way out if he's still unwilling to turn off the juice: He can turn to the weird stuff on MTV and wait for his parents to make him turn off the set.

23

THE REAL KIDS' EMMYS

Best Comedy: "Laverne and Shirley"

Best Comedy Outside of "Laverne and Shirley": "Happy Days"

Best Comedy Using People from "Happy Days": "Joanie Loves Chachi"

Best Comedy Not about Stuff from the Fifties: "Three's Company"

Best Program about Stuff from the Fifties that's not a Comedy: "Boone"

Best Program that Really Was from the Fifties: "Leave It to Beaver"

Best Program on at 9:00 P.M. on Wednesday: "The Facts of Life"

Best Comedy with Kids in it: "Diff'rent Strokes"

Best Comedy with Only One Kid in It: "Webster"

Best Comedy with No Kids in It: "M*A*S*H"

Best Comedy that Isn't Funny: "Silver Spoons"

Best Program that Isn't a Comedy but Is Funny: "Love Boat"

Best Cartoon: "Scooby Doo"

Best Old Cartoon: "Road Runner"

Best New Cartoon: "Monchhichis"

Best Program that's like Cartoons but Isn't a Cartoon: "The Muppets"

Best Program about Dumb Kids in a High School: "Welcome Back Kotter"

Best Program about Smart Kids in a High School: "Fame"

Best Action Show: "The A-Team"

Best Show that Used to Be the Best Action Show: "The Dukes of Hazzard"

Best Action Show Where People Can Really Get Hurt: "That's Incredible"

Best Program on Cable: "You Can't Do That on Television"

Best Program on After the News: "Family Feud"

Best Program on when "Family Feud" Isn't on After the News: "In Search of . . ." (especially the Bermuda Triangle)

Best Program with a Judge in It: "The People's Court"

Best Program with a Chimp in it: "Mr. Smith"

Best Program Your Parents Watch but Don't Like for You To: "Dallas"

Best Program on at 9:00 P.M. on Sunday: Anything except "Masterpiece Theatre"

Best Program that Started Out as a Toy: "He-Man and the Masters of the Universe"

Best Program that Started Out as a Toy that's Still Better than the Program: "Smurfs"

24　THE REAL KIDS' READING LIST

All the experts are ready to explain why Johnny Can't Read. And the answer most commonly offered is that Johnny watches too much television.

The truth is, Johnny can read—and does. Moreover, he reads mainly *while* he watches television. *What* he reads is a different story.

Real Kids read:

—comic books
—cereal boxes (back and side panels)
— *TV Guide*
—other people's mail
—whatever their parents tell them not to

In fairness, Real Kids also read books now and then. Here, selection runs to books with lots of pictures—especially of Robby Benson or Kristy McNichol—or anybody—in the movie version. Occasionally, Real Kids will read a book without pictures—but only to find the dirty parts. Real Kids don't read any periodical except *TV Guide*. They don't read *Junior Scholastic* (though they may do the puzzles). And they don't read any magazine labeled "For Children." While waiting at the dentist's office, Real Kids may thumb through back issues of

National Geographic to look for naked people. Unlike some *Playboy* readers, however, Real Kids make no pretense of being interested in the articles. Of course, Real Kids don't read homework assignments.

Finally, Real Kids don't read long paragraphs.

25 REAL KIDS AT PLAY: LONG DAY'S JOURNEY INTO NIGHT

See Dick run? See him jump, fall, kick, punch, smash, break, wreck, demolish?

In the limited time left them after terrorizing their teachers, ruining family mealtimes, and playing arpeggios on the cable box, Real Kids will wear you out cruising a million miles an hour through their various and sundry Real Kid activities. Then, when you figure they ought to be ready to sag quietly in front of a TV set like so many zombie adults, they wear you out complaining, "There's nothing to do."

The more you insist that they're really just tired, the more frantic they become. And with reason. The truth is, Real Kids don't get tired. They get bored. And they stay bored until they pass into that state of Real Kid Nirvana known as Overtired, in which, seeming to grow extra limbs to flail at priceless heirlooms, they do their best imitation of Linda Blair in *The Exorcist*. As a result, experienced parents generally prefer their Real Kids out throwing empty beer cans onto the highway to Real Kids bored and on their hands.

Sensing a nearly hopeless state of affairs, parents of Real Kids sometimes panic and try to get inventive, suggesting some outlet for all that Real Kid drive. Mom suggests Dad might take junior out to the course to try his hand at golf. Outpourings of Real Kid joy, eagerness,

Gee, the kids are awfully quiet . . . do you think
we should count our blessings or dig out the
homeowners policy?

gratitude, enthusiasm. Don't be fooled. Real Kids accept the invitation enthusiastically. Then, twenty paces from tee-off, they're begging to hold the clubs. Twenty paces more and they're complaining the clubs are too heavy. By the time you reach the first hole they utter their first "There's nothing to do." And they alternate this with "This is boring" and asking you why you "keep saying 'four'" through every stroke of a nine- or eighteen-hole course—if you are masochist enough to give them that much opportunity.

It's easy to avoid such needless torture if one but remembers the many activities included among the "nothings" in a Real Kid's nothing-to-do. Real Kids don't play golf. Period. They won't even watch it on TV.

They don't play squash either. Or racquetball. Or paddleball.

Real Kids don't play chess, or cribbage, or honeymoon bridge. They don't understand why they can't use the backgammon set to play miniature shuffleboard.

To get them to go to museums (the ones with dinosaur bones excluded), Real Kids must be forced. They *cannot* be forced to go to art galleries. The longest concert a Real Kid will tolerate is when the glee club sings the "Star Spangled Banner," and even then only up to the part about the "rocketsredglare."

Real Kids are bad tourists. They don't see why they should drive or ride or fly for five hours to go someplace where they don't even have a Chuck E Cheese and you can get only three stations on the TV—one of which goes up-and-down because the "vertical hold" doesn't.

Real Kids do no more than three of the activities listed in any of those books with names like *1001 Ways to Amuse Your Child*.

Real Kids never finish anything in arts and crafts. They don't write letters to the president. Or to the mayor. Or to Konstantin Chernenko. Real Kids write only once to their Third World pen pals.

Real Kids don't take walks (unless they're headed for the candy store or a Carvel ice cream store). They don't keep diaries for more than a week at a time. (Seven days' entries of "June —th. Had pizza for dinner" are at least six days too many.) Real Kids don't earn merit badges. And they don't "do projects."

You want us to guess what it was going to be?

A parent at wit's end might remind himself that there is an infinity of things Real Kids *do*—without any prompting and despite any warnings. Thus, Real Kids:

> play Old Maid, play Spit, play War;
> play Monopoly, cheat at Monopoly, cheat at War;
> play running bases—or, better still, Monkey-in-the-Middle—with a hapless younger sibling;
> collect things;
> break things;
> do stuff in the snow;
> start model airplanes;
> start lanyards;
> start potholders;
> make clay ashtrays that are doomed to explode in the kiln;
> try to do Rubik's Cube;
> try to cheat at Rubik's Cube;
> break Rubik's Cube;
> do any of the above while watching television;
> go hiking (provided sufficient refreshments are brought along);
> tell ethnic jokes they don't get;
> write dirty words with the Scrabble pieces or insist that *zegex* is a word they got wrong in the spelling bee;
> write dirty words in freshly poured cement. (Any kid will etch his initials in cement; only Real Kids, however, see it as the perfect medium for calligraphy, autobiography, investigative reporting, and smut.)
> are ingenious at finding things to do after they're sent to bed.

Finally, two pieces of advice for truly desperate parents:

—Real Kids don't talk to child psychologists.
—And they don't use the B-tickets at Disneyworld.

26 THE NATIONAL PASTIME, REAL KID DIVISION

No book on Real Kids would be complete without a word about Little League. Of course, a lot of Real Kids play in Little League. But Little League is not the Real Kids' sport. If there is a Real Kids' sport, it is probably running bases—or tag, or maybe dodgeball, or kick the can.

What Little League is, is the sport of Real Kids' parents. A lot of Real Kids who don't think their parents were ever really kids—and certainly not Real Kids—find out different at Little League games. Little League games may not always bring out the Real Kid in Real Kids, but they definitely bring out the Real Kid in Real Parents.

27 SIX THINGS TO DO WITH A RUBBER BAND

1) Shoot it at your younger sister/brother.

2) Shoot it at your older sister/brother.

3) Wear it around your wrist to:
   a) cut off the circulation,
   b) turn your hand red,
   c) make "marks" you can feel when you take it off.

4) Stretch it till it breaks.

5) Stuff it in a drawer somewhere with a lot of other rubber bands.

6) Chew it.

28

A REAL KID AND HIS PET

A Real Kid needs a pet. And he will make this need very clear—very often—to petless parents. A Real Kid doesn't understand mitigating circumstances such as three-room apartments, newborn babies, chronic asthma, or transatlantic travel. A pet is a need. It is nonnegotiable.

Almost any pet will do: a gerbil, a snake, a hermit crab. In a pinch a Real Kid can even get some mileage out of a solitary lightning bug in a mayonnaise jar with two holes punched in the top (at least until it stops glowing and loses the will to keep beating its brains against the glass).

In the course of growing up, a Real Kid usually becomes the proud owner of several different pets in succession (usually rapid), as one by one each little charge flourishes briefly and meets its inevitable though untimely end, to be either buried in a shoe box or flushed down the W.C. in accordance with the wishes of the bereaved. The truth is, Real Kids don't take care of pets.

They especially don't take care of turtles. One week and three successful "the-turtle's-gone" searches after its initial purchase, a Real Kid's turtle is generally found shell-down on his colored pebbles, suffering visibly from dehydration and overextended neck muscles. The fate of painted turtles is even more grotesque. These dandy little show-and-tell items usually turn up at laundry-folding time, stuck in a wad of tissue in a jacket pocket. It is not a pretty sight.

I'm sure the cat didn't mean to scratch you it was only frightened when you turned on the hedge clippers.

Real Kids torture cats. When a Real Kid locks himself in the bathroom, odds are there's a muffled cat terrified out of its wits in there with him.

Real Kids like tropical fish for a day-and-a-half. During this time they go through the feeding ritual maybe fifty or a hundred times—mostly without using any food—in order to see the fish rush to the top of the tank with open mouths and then sink disappointedly to the bottom when they realize nothing is falling from those stubby Real Kid fingers. Then after a course of experimentation that would have made Pavlov blush, Real Kids never go near the tank again, with food or without.

Real Kids like parakeets only in Woolworth's. Actually, Real Kids are more interested in those little wooden swings, plastic balls, and birdseed bells than they are in the birds themselves and aren't all that troubled by a pet bird's sudden demise or disappearance as long as they've still got a cageful of all that cute stuff.

Despite all this, Real Kids love their pets. And they cry like—well, like Real Kids—when a beloved pet meets his maker, whether through starvation, terror-induced cardiac arrest, or unanticipated entry into the vacuum cleaner (how else do you clean a canary?).

Above all others, Real Kids love dogs—because they're big and dumb and don't get mad even when you "try things" on them. Except poodles. Real Kids hate poodles. It's mutual.

Finally one point worth remembering: Behind every Real Kid with a living pet is a parent dishing out the fishmeal, setting up the plastic palm trees, cleaning the cages, buying the cuttlebones, repairing the treadmills, sifting through the kitty litter, and walking the dog, walking the dog, walking the dog, walking the dog.

29

RELATIVITY

There are a few relatives Real Kids like:

    grandparents
    parents (now and then)
    cousins with videogames

And a lot they don't:

    older siblings
    younger siblings
    uncles with mustaches
    aunts with mustaches
    uncles who pinch
    aunts with wet lips
    aunts and uncles who are younger than they are
    cousins (note exception above)

Real Kids love visiting their grandparents. Especially at mealtime. Even Real Kids who refuse to eat anything but Frosted Flakes and Hawaiian Punch at home dive with a vengeance into pots of unidentifiable stuff "grandma made" that looks and smells as if it'd been pressure-cooked continuously since their last visit. And then get granddad to take them to McDonald's.

The first thing a Real Kid does at his aunt's house is scan the room for the breakables. Usually he can target five or six of these before your average aunt wises up and sticks the rest of the stuff—or the Real Kid—in the basement.

If a Real Kid should sit quietly on the sofa for a minute or two when visiting an aunt, it usually means he's found a clearance between it and the wall, suitable for dropping "things" where nobody will find them.

A Real Kid wants to check out all his cousin's toys. He likes to play with the ones he doesn't have at home. He also likes to play with the ones he does have at home—and hasn't looked at in several years. Especially if these are the ones his cousin wants to use at the moment.

Real Kids resent being forced to get dressed up to go sit around with a beer-drinking uncle in a tee-shirt planted in front of a wrestling match on "Wide World of Sports." And they resent more being forced to get dressed up to go sit around at their cousin's wedding.

The only thing Real Kids never resent about their relatives is not being invited to visit them. And they're willing to go to some lengths to insure that this will be the case.

30

REAL KIDS
ON MUSIC

Noise. Garbage. Filth.

When it comes to appraising musical taste, some adults tend to lump all those under twenty together. They figure all kids listen to the same junk, whether they're seven or seventeen. Untrue. Real Kids listen to their own special junk, and it's usually a notch or two junkier than the stuff teenagers listen to.

Years back, it was Real Kids who put "Oo-ee-oo-ah-ah" and "Greasy Kid Stuff" on the charts when their older brothers and sisters were just getting into late Chuck Berry, middle Presley, and early Stones. Real Kids wore out the grooves on "Yellow Polka Dot Bikini" and were the only people who knew—or cared—that it had a sequel on the flip side.

Unlike their teenage brothers and sisters, Real Kids don't argue when their parents call the music they listen to "noise." Real Kids like noise. The noisier the better.

Real Kids like musical groups with zoological names: Monkees, Beatles, Stray Cats, Def Leppard. But even better, they like musical groups with a zoological sound. Like the Chipmunks. Real Kids can listen to Chipmunk gold endlessly. And when they run out of authentic Chipmunk hits to get off on, they create their own by playing the Everly Brothers or the Lennon Sisters or Police on the wrong speed.

Real Kids like groups who dress up—like cowboys, cops, vampires, perverts. Somehow it just sounds better when the musicians don't look like musicians—maybe because it fits better with music that doesn't sound like music.

Real Kids don't get misty over the "old standards." They like new music, which they then proceed to "age" fast, like by playing "Eye of the Tiger" an average of fifty times per day for a month and a half.

Real Kids don't "dig the big band sound." They think the "Chattanooga Choo-Choo" is the train Dinah was caught in the kitchen of with someone in "I've Been Working on the Railroad." To Real Kids, "Stardust" is another name for that drug Robert Blake keeps haranguing them about not taking from shady strangers in the schoolyard. Real Kids think "Smoke Gets in Your Eyes" was written by Henny Youngman. As a joke.

Real Kids don't hum. And they don't listen to anything they could.

Some parents, hoping to stave off the inevitable, try brainwashing their offspring with classical recordings and music lessons, generally on instruments like the viola, the accordian, or one of those organs they're always giving as prizes on "The Price Is Right." A Real Kid will rise above such maneuvers. If nominated, he will not play. If elected, he will not learn.

Real Kids don't practice. They don't play scales. They leave their instruments behind in gym lockers or, better still, on the bus seat on the way to a music lesson. And they have done more than Reaganomics to send scores of music teachers back to school to learn a trade.

Parents learn hard. They sit through week after week of torturous half hours, dropping $1,700 in clarinet lessons, and then one day, EEEWHEEEooooREEEP——GLANGGG'! Mozart gets plugged into an amp and the electric minuet is born.

Real Kids don't play classical music. They won't even stay in the same room when it's on. And that goes for all the classics: Bach, Beethoven, Brahms, Webern, Wagner, Welk, and Guy Lombardo. The only highbrow musical event Real Kids ever wanted tickets to was the "Diet Coke" concert. And then only so they could get to see Telly Savalas.

Real Kids don't like the slow parts. They don't like motets, quintets, quartets, or clorets. They don't like any instrument with fewer than six strings. And two amps. And 200 decibels.

Real Kids like music with drums. And cymbals. And cannons. And atomic bombs. They like music adults mistake for natural disasters.

Now Walkman has made it possible for grownups to tune up their Mendelssohn and Mantovani while junior's hearing gradually succumbs to the palpable strains of the Grateful Dead mainlined into his eardrum. A mistake. The only way adults will ever get Real Kids to listen to what they call music is to start playing "Maniac" or "Sex and Seventeen" themselves—and singing along, if possible. For above all else, Real Kid music must pass one "acid" test: to be screamingly unbearable to anyone over 21.

When they've got that Walkman on, they don't hear a thing . . . unless you whisper.

31 PEOPLE, PLACES, AND THINGS: WHAT INTERESTS REAL KIDS

Places of Interest to Real Kids

The North Pole
The South Pole
Metropolis
Krypton
Dodge City
Gotham City
Surf City
The Amazon
Disneyland
Disneyworld
Mars
Oz
Other planets, solar systems, galaxies, etc.

Places of No Interest to Real Kids

Paris (London, Rome, Brussels, etc.)
The Near East
The Far East
The Middle East
The Northeast
Cleveland

People of Interest to Real Kids

Marco Polo (mainly because of that great game he
    made up)
Davy Crockett
Farrah Fawcett
Elvis Presley
George Washington
    } (Anybody who gets them a day off
Abraham Lincoln } from school has to be pretty great.)
The Lone Ranger
Tonto
Sherlock Holmes (despite the violin)
Dr. Watson
The Wright Brothers
The Smith Brothers
The Doobie Brothers
Robin Hood
Maid Marion
Betsy Ross
Dolly Madison (They'd like to know what she did to get
    an ice cream named after her.)
Betty Crocker

People of No Interest to Real Kids

Freud
Gandhi } (If no one remembers their first names, they
Garbo } couldn't be all that great.)
Sargent Shriver (even worse than no first name)
Peter the Great (If you have to tell them you're great,
    you're probably not so great.)
Sir Thomas More (*Nobody's* interested in Sir Thomas
    More.)
Oliver Wendell Holmes (Just no match for his brother
    Sherlock.)
Jayne Meadows (You ask for Steve Allen, you *want* Steve
    Allen.)
Jack Paar
Dick Cavett

Events of Interest to Real Kids

The Sinking of the *Titanic*
The Battle of the Alamo
Custer's Last Stand
The Gunfight at the OK-Corral
The Parting of the Red Sea (preferably the Charlton Heston version)
Alexander Graham Bell's telling Mr. Watson to "Come here, I want you."
Blowing up Death Star
The Great Leap Forward (or whatever that Armstrong guy said when he stepped on the moon)
The day they were born
The day they got cable

Events of No Interest to Real Kids

World War I
The Middle Ages (also the Renaissance, the Enlightenment, the Jazz Age, etc.)
VE Day
VJ Day
Arbor Day
The Good Old Days

32

A REAL KIDS' MISCELLANY

Real Kids' likes and dislikes that defy categorization include the items below.

Things Real Kids Like

Rides their older siblings like
Rides their parents hate
Checking out what's going on in the other cars at drive-in movies
Being the first kid on the block with a toy, pet, or contagious disease
Being the only one in a place (like a lake, a bus, a condemned building)
Going into a place so another kid can't be the only one in it
Sleeping over
Playing in the snow
Cereals with prizes inside
Cereals shaped like pastries
Cereals advertised on Saturday morning cartoon shows

Things Real Kids Don't Like

Rides their younger siblings like
Slow slides
Taking photographs with their family (though they're somehow always popping up in total strangers' photographs)
Sleeping in (especially on Sunday)
Shoveling snow (except when they get paid for it)
Shopping
Shoemen
Shredded Wheat

33 FIVE THINGS REAL KIDS BOTH LIKE AND DISLIKE

1) Their first names

2) Their last names

3) Going to bed

4) Being scared

5) Their parents

34

A REAL KID PHRASE BOOK

For some time now, to appreciate Real Kid conversation, there has been one essential to bear in mind: To register approval of a movie, a Smurf sticker, a best friend, a pair of leg warmers—or of anything at all for that matter—there are only three indispensable entries in the lexicon. The first is "excellent." The second is "really excellent." The third is "totally excellent."

Thus, an excellent house is one that has boxes of excellent cookies kept at arm's reach in the kitchen and a really excellent video game or two in the family room. The Real Kid long on praise and short on time can substitute *ex* without compromising either his approval or his integrity.

Of course, occasionally even Real Kids feel the need for an additional plaudit or two (like for telling someone about all the excellent stuff on last night's "Dukes of Hazzard"). "Decent" is one alternative, as in "It was de-cent." Ditto "terrif." Or, for those moments of near tongue-tied sublimity, a Real Kid can still fall comfortably back on "Oh, wow!" or "awesome."

The list of negative Real Kidwords, on the other hand, is virtually endless—and largely unprintable. The printables include: dumb, gross, weird, stupid, sick, yecchy, pukey, dopey, junky, creepy, crumby, crappy, dogbreath, scuzzball, the pits.

Real Kids also seem to need lots of ways to express disbelief (c.f. Real Kid Ethics). Thus, the skeptical Real Kid can call someone "a fraud" or just tell him to "try again" or "bag his face." Most tall-tale tellers will pack it in after the sixth "not really."

It is worth noting that, here in the 1980s, Real Kids don't say (in addition to the perennial "please") lots of words once prominent in the Real Kidictionary, to wit: swell, cool, hip, swift, groovy, fab, dy-no-mite. Real Kids will use no slang beyond its time.

In addition to these essentials there are a few phrases no Real Kid goes more than a few hours—or maybe minutes—without using:

Me too.
Me first.
No. Now!
It's not fair. (especially in sibling relationships)
Quit it.
She/He started it.
I hate you. (best reserved for parents)
Move!
Let me do it! Let me do it! (usually followed, after a
    short pause, by a muffled request for help)

Some parents nowadays are concerned about their Real Kids going around being everything: "I be tired; I be getting home late this afternoon; that Mr. T be one excellent guy." Real Kids just don't see why they should bother with good English when a few years from now all they'll need is FORTRAN.

35 WHAT REAL KIDS WANT TO BE WHEN THEY GROW UP

a policeman
a fireman
a nurse
a stewardess
a pilot
an astronaut
a race car driver
a bus driver
a movie star
a ball player
a ball boy
Robin Hood
a secret agent
a toy store owner
a candy store owner
a captain of something
a VIP
an MVP
a model
a mommy

And What They
Don't Want to Be

a principal
a shoeman
a CPA
a Ph.D.
a librarian
a Liberian
a dermatologist
an opthalmologist
a congressman from anywhere
an ambassador to anywhere
a real estate salesman
a notary public
a mortician
a druggist
a dentist
a daddy

36

TWO THINGS
REAL KIDS WANT
TO DO BUT CAN'T

Drive.

Shave (face or legs, depending on sex).

I guess this means I'll have to revise the 'birds and bees' speech I've been practicing since he was born.

37

REAL PARENTS

There are a lot of people going off to father-son dinners and mother-daughter luncheons these days, showing off the handiwork with which they were regaled on Mother's or Father's Day, and proudly calling themselves parents. They may be parents, but they're not Real Parents. The only Real Parents are the parents of Real Kids—and they never confess to it willingly.

It's easy to distinguish the genuine article: Real Parents are too embarrassed to go to parenting seminars. Or the PTA. Or the supermarket.

Real Parents don't look forward to Open School Night. They shudder every time they get a communiqué on official school stationery. Real Parents know better than to ask their kids how they're doing at school. They do their kids' homework, even though they know they're doing it wrong, on the presumption that wrong homework is better than no homework at all.

Real Parents are the only people who can read the cards their kids make them. Or recognize the wallets they make them as wallets. Real Parents put their kids' artwork up on the refrigerator—to protect the finish on the refrigerator. Then they pray that none of their guests will come into the kitchen.

Real Parents may tell friends they're trying to choose

between sending their kids to Yale or State, but secretly pray they won't join the Moonies. Or the Mob.

A Real Parent blames the other parent—or Dr. Spock. Or both. He fantasizes about losing child custody suits. He feels sorry for Dustin Hoffman at the *end* of *Kramer vs. Kramer*.

Real Parents don't look forward to summer. Or to Christmas. Or to weekends. Or to dinner.

They buy their kids a TV of their own. Or whatever else it takes to keep them in their rooms.

They sacrifice to send them off to sleep-away camp. A place that will get their kids out of the house for eight weeks is easily worth half-a-year's salary.

Real Parents are sure kids were different when they were Real Kids. Or at least that's what they tell their kids.

They have no argument with W. C. Fields except that they think he may have been a little hard on dogs.

Finally, Real Parents read books like *Real Kids Don't Say Please*. And write them.

38

THE REAL KIDS' FINAL EXAM

1. Your aunt comes to your house to visit and brings a box of chocolates. You:

   a) sit patiently until you're offered.
   b) ask if you can please have one.
   c) steal a few when no one's looking.
   d) get your cousin to steal a few when no one's looking.

2. You haven't done your homework and the teacher is coming down the aisle. You:

   a) try to copy the homework from the kid in front of you.
   b) try to buy the homework from the kid in front of you.
   c) tell the teacher your little brother destroyed your homework.
   d) tell the teacher the kid in front of you destroyed your homework.
   e) cry.

3. Which of these presents did you ask for on your last birthday?

   a) a bicycle
   b) a dog
   c) an Erector set
   d) a new coat
   e) a, b, and c only
   f) all of the above

4. Which of the following have you nagged your parents to take you to in the past year?

    a) Disneyland
    b) Disneyworld
    c) Your cousin's house
    d) Six Flags
    e) The Picasso Exhibit at the Museum of Modern Art
    f) a, b, d, and a wax museum

5. How many times were you absent in the past month?

    a) none
    b) once
    c) twice
    d) three or four maybe
    e) counting Fridays?

Scoring:

1. **a)** 0 points; **b)** -1 point; **c)** 5 points; **d)** 10 points (add 5 if your cousin isn't a Real Kid).
2. **a)** 5 points; **b)** 10 points; **c)** 15 points; **d)** 20 points; **e)** 25 points (Real Kids do cry when it's convenient).
3. **a)** 10 points; **b)** 10 points; **c)** 5 points; **d)** 0 points; **e)** 20 points **f)** 1 point (Real Kids just don't ask for new coats).
4. **a)** 10 points; **b)** 10 points; **c)** 1 point; **d)** 10 points; **e)** -5 points; **f)** 20 points.
5. **a)** 0 points; **b)** 1 point; **c)** 2 points; **d)** 10 points; **e)** 20 points.

How to read your score:

100 = A bona fide Real Kid. Anything less than **100** = A please-sayer: Real Kids cheat.

Tissue Engineering of Temporomandibular Joint Cartilage

Synthesis Lectures on Tissue Engineering

Editor
Kyriacos A. Athanasiou, *University of California at Davis*

Tissue Engineering of Temporomandibular Joint Cartilage
Kyriacos A. Athanasiou, Alejandro A. Almarza, Michael S. Detamore, and Kerem N. Kalpakci
2009

Engineering the Knee Meniscus
Kyriacos A. Athanasiou and Johannah Sanchez-Adams
2009

Copyright © 2009 by Morgan & Claypool

Tissue Engineering of Temporomandibular Joint Cartilage

Kyriacos A. Athanasiou, Alejandro A. Almarza, Michael S. Detamore, and Kerem N. Kalpakci

www.morganclaypool.com

ISBN: 9781598299960   paperback
ISBN: 9781598299977   ebook

DOI 10.2200/S00198ED1V01Y200906TIS002

A Publication in the Morgan & Claypool Publishers series
SYNTHESIS LECTURES ON TISSUE ENGINEERING

Lecture #2
Series Editor: Kyriacos A. Athanasiou, University of California at Davis

Series ISSN
Synthesis Lectures on Tissue Engineering
Print 1944-0316   Electronic 1944-0308

Tissue Engineering of Temporomandibular Joint Cartilage

Kyriacos A. Athanasiou
University of California at Davis

Alejandro A. Almarza
University of Pittsburgh and McGowan Institute

Michael S. Detamore
University of Kansas

Kerem N. Kalpakci
Rice University

SYNTHESIS LECTURES ON TISSUE ENGINEERING #2

MORGAN & CLAYPOOL PUBLISHERS

ABSTRACT

The temporomandibular joint (TMJ) is a site of intense morbidity for millions of people, especially young, pre-menopausal women. Central to TMJ afflictions are the cartilaginous tissues of the TMJ, especially those of the disc and condylar cartilage, which play crucial roles in normal function of this unusual joint. Damage or disease to these tissues significantly impacts a patient's quality of life by making common activities such as talking and eating difficult and painful. Unfortunately, these tissues have limited ability to heal, necessitating the development of treatments for repair or replacement. The burgeoning field of tissue engineering holds promise that replacement tissues can be constructed in the laboratory to recapitulate the functional requirements of native tissues. This book outlines the biomechanical, biochemical, and anatomical characteristics of the disc and condylar cartilage, and also provides a historical perspective of past and current TMJ treatments and previous tissue engineering efforts. This book was written to serve as a reference for researchers seeking to learn about the TMJ, for undergraduate and graduate level courses, and as a compendium of TMJ tissue engineering design criteria.

KEYWORDS

temporomandibular joint, tissue engineering, TMJ disc, mandibular condyle, cartilage, fibrocartilage, chondrocyte, fibrochondrocyte, temporomandibular joint dysfunction (TMD), biomechanics

Dedicated to all my brilliant PhD students,
past and present, for perpetually challenging
not only my research but my entire philosophy
on life. It is for these people that
I am in academics and it is these graduate
students who always inspire me. —KA^2

To my mother, Zulay, and my father, Dario,
for your love and dedication that have made
it possible for me to achieve anything
I dreamed. To Sabrina, for your love and support,
without which the journey would not be worth taking. —Alejandro

To my wife, Leslie, for being my guiding light and
my number one supporter.
To Dr. Milind Singh and Dr. Limin Wang, whose work was
the foundation of my group's work in mandibular condyle
characterization and regeneration.
And to my parents, Scott and Lynne, and parents-in-law,
Henry and Wilma, for their guidance and support. —Michael

Dedicated to Mom and Baba for your unending commitment
to my sisters and me. To Nevin and Allison, for your companionship
and understanding. To my parents-in-law,
Shelley and Dave, for your love and support.
And to my wife, Jessica, for your true and unbounded love. —Kerem

Contents

Preface

The goal for this book was to gather current knowledge related to engineering of TMJ cartilage into a single cohesive work. We feel that the writing style and illustrations render the book accessible to those with only minimal background on the subject, while the quantitative aspects will aid those already practicing in the field. The book begins by introducing the joint as a whole, including its anatomy, biomechanical environment, development, and also its pathophysiology and current treatments. In Chapters 2 and 3, the specific cartilages of interest for tissue engineers, namely the disc and condylar cartilage, are characterized in terms of their anatomical, biochemical, biomechanical, and cellular properties. Chapters 4 and 5 discuss previous work engineering the disc and condylar cartilage *in vitro*, highlighting the crucial aspects of these endeavors. The book finishes with recommendations for the future of TMJ tissue engineering, including the use of stem cells, specific design standards, and methods for the functional assessment of tissue engineered constructs. We feel that both university students and researchers will benefit from this information in their study of the TMJ and tissue engineering. Our hope is that future researchers will use this resource as a starting point and that their work will ultimately lead to improved patient outcomes.

Kyriacos A. Athanasiou, Alejandro A. Almarza, Michael S. Detamore, and Kerem N. Kalpakci
University of California at Davis
March 2009

CHAPTER 1

The Temporomandibular Joint

Table 1.1: Table of Abbreviations			
APC	Antigen presenting cells	MHC	Major histocompatibility complex
ASTM	American Society for Testing and Materials	MEM	Minimum essential medium
bFGF	Basic fibroblast growth factor	MMP	Matrix metalloproteinases
BMP-2	Bone morphogenetic protein-2	PCL	Polycaprolactone
CAD	Computer assisted design	PDGF	Platelet derived growth factor
CC	Costal chondrocytes	PGA	Polyglycolic acid
CT	Computerized tomography	PLA/PGA	Polylactic acid/polyglycolic acid
DF	Dermal fibroblast	PLGA	Poly(lactic-co-glycolic acid)
EB	Embryoid body	PLLA	Poly-L-lactic-acid
ECM	Extracellular matrix	PMMA	Polymethylmethacrylate
ELISA	Enzyme-linked immunosorbent assay	RT	Reverse transcription
ePTFE	Expanded polytetrafluoroethylene	rt-PCR	Real-time polymerase chain reaction
FDA	Food and Drug Administration	SDS	Sodium dodecyl sulfate
Fos-LI	Fos-like immunoreactivity	SEM	Scanning electron microscopy
G-HCl	Guanidine hydrochloride	SLS	Selective laser sintering
GAG	Glycosaminoglycan	TGF-$\beta1$, $\beta3$	Transforming growth factor-$\beta1$, $\beta3$
H&E	Hematoxylin and eosin	TMB	3,3',5,5'-Tetramethylbenzidine
HBSS	Hanks' balanced salt solution	TMD	Temporomandibular disorder
hESC	Human embryonic stem cell	TMJ	Temporomandibular joint
IGF-1	Insulin-like growth factor-1	TNF	Tissue necrosis factor
IL-1,2	Interleukin-1, 2	UHMWPE	Ultra-high molecular weight polyethylene

1.1 TISSUE ENGINEERING

The lack of an intrinsic regenerative ability in cartilaginous tissues renders them ideal candidates for tissue engineering approaches. The field of musculoskeletal tissue engineering focuses on producing tissue replacements with suitable biomechanical and structural properties through the use of natural and synthetic materials. In general, tissue engineering approaches utilize the interaction of cells, scaffolds, biological signals, and bioreactors.

The choice of cell source is fundamental in the tissue engineering process. A clinically feasible cell source should be abundant, healthy, and leave little donor site morbidity [1]. Selection of an alternative source must also consider the functionality of the cells. A myriad of cell sources can be used for cartilaginous tissue engineering, such as native cartilage cells from the autologous site, or cartilage cells from a different joint. Further, mesenchymal stem cells from different sources, such as bone marrow, fat, muscle, or periodontal tissues, could be differentiated to cartilage.

The type of scaffolding used will have a profound impact on outcomes. Hydrogels have proven to be the scaffolding choice in numerous tissue engineering applications. Alginate and agarose hydrogels are two popular natural hydrogels used in cartilage tissue engineering. Non-woven meshes of synthetic polymers have also seen success in cartilage tissue engineering. A popular choice, polyglycolic acid (PGA), has seen encouraging results for cartilage tissue engineering [2]–[4]. A scaffoldless approach has also been proposed, where cartilage cells self-assemble in a mold to produce cartilage tissue analogues *in vitro* [5].

Biological signals can activate pathways that cascade into extracellular matrix (ECM) protein production to recapitulate the native tissues [6]. Growth factors are the most common biological signals utilized in tissue engineering; however, chemicals such as ascorbic acid, proline, and glutamine can also serve as signals. Further, genetic engineering can be used to express these and other therapeutic agents within the cells.

Mechanical force may also be applied during the culturing process to produce a phenotypically correct tissue with proper extracellular matrix alignment, which is often obtained through the use of bioreactors. Four main types of forces are currently used in cartilage-culturing processes: hydrostatic pressure, direct compression, "high-shear" fluid environments, and "low-shear" fluid environments.

Specifically, for the temporomandibular joint (TMJ), tissue engineering investigations of its two major structures (the disc and the condyle) have been conducted independent of one another. Both the condyle and disc tissue-engineering communities have made significant advances in recent years, although the investigations on the disc began much earlier. Four TMJ disc tissue engineering studies were published from 1991 to 2001 [7]–[10], and while important issues were addressed, such as cell source, biomaterials, and shape specific scaffolds, the common theme among these pioneering studies was an unfamiliarity with the available characterization data for the TMJ disc in terms of cell content and matrix composition.

In 2001, strategies for TMJ tissue engineering, including cell sources, scaffolding materials, and signaling, were reviewed [11], and a photopolymerization method for developing a shape-specific TMJ disc scaffold was developed [12, 13]. Although, it was not until three years later that the next effort of TMJ disc tissue-engineering studies were published, all of which utilized cells derived from the TMJ disc. Most of these studies were from Athanasiou's group, which collectively supported the use of PGA non-woven meshes over agarose gels [2], while promoting the spinner flask as the preferred seeding method with PGA scaffolds. They also demonstrated the importance of using growth factors such as insulin-like growth factor-I [14, 15], and recommended 25 μg/mL as a preferred ascorbic acid concentration [16]. Athanasiou's group also revealed the detrimental effects of passaging and pellet culture [17], and investigated the effects of hydrostatic pressure [18] and rotating wall bioreactors [19]. In 2006, another study suggested the use of platelet derived growth factor-BB in the culturing of TMJ disc cells for tissue engineering approaches [20]. These and other TMJ disc tissue engineering studies are reviewed in detail in Chapter 4.

Unlike the TMJ disc, mandibular condyle/ramus tissue engineering studies did not appear in the literature until the year 2000. The two early leading groups in the field were those of Mao and Hollister. The approach by Mao and colleagues [21]–[23] involved encapsulating marrow-derived mesenchymal stem cells in a polyethylene glycol diacrylate hydrogel to create stratified bone and cartilage layers in the shape of a human condyle. On the other hand, Hollister's group [24]–[27] developed a strategy for producing person-specific condyle-shaped scaffolds based on computed tomography and/or magnetic resonance images coupled with solid free-form fabrication (layer by layer printing). Greater detail on these and other mandibular condyle tissue engineering efforts can be found in Chapter 5.

1.2 ANATOMY AND PHYSIOLOGY OF THE TEMPORO-MANDIBULAR JOINT

As reviewed elsewhere [28], the TMJ is a synovial, bilateral, ginglymo-diarthrodial joint, and it is formed by the articulation of the condyle of the mandible against the glenoid fossa and articular eminence of the temporal bone (Figure 1.1) [29, 30]. The mandible with its condyles is the major moving bone of the TMJ. Each condyle is composed of bone covered by a unique cartilage layer. The region of the mandible immediately inferior to the condylar head is referred to as the ramus. On the temporal bone, the anterior ridge of the glenoid fossa merges with the posterior slope of the eminence. The fossa is the other major articulating surface of the TMJ, but it remains stationary with respect to the cranium. A fibrocartilaginous disc is situated between the condyle and fossa-eminence, generally oriented between the transverse and coronal planes (Figure 1.2). The TMJ disc and its attachments separate the joint space into superior and inferior compartments.

While this nomenclature suggests that the disc is isolated from its superior and inferior relationships by true "spaces," under normal functional conditions, the distances are extremely small and filled with synovial fluid [29]. This arrangement allows the fibrocartilaginous disc to fill the void between the condylar head and the glenoid fossa, promoting congruity between two dissimilarly shaped and sized structures [31] (Figure 1.2).

The disc spans the condylar head and together with its peripheral attachments and surrounding joint capsule, produces a closed space separating intra-articular and extra-articular environments. Three morphological zones have been described for the disc [30], which can be observed in a sagittal view of the TMJ (Figure 1.3). The thickest region of the disc is the posterior band, followed by the anterior band. The intermediate zone represents the thinnest portion of the disc. The junctions between the zones are indistinguishable by gross examination and appear to blend with each other. In a sagittal section, the disc has been described as manifesting a biconcave shape, but this is not an entirely accurate depiction of its morphology. It is attached along its entire peripheral margin to both the condylar neck and the cranial base through a variety of different connective tissues. The superior attachments are less tenuous and allow the condylar head to slide forward and from side

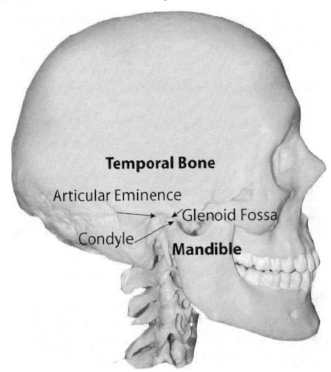

Figure 1.1: Bony structures of the TMJ.

to side in relation to the fossa during movements of the joint. Medially and laterally, the superior surface of the disc turns inferiorly before blending with fibers of the capsule. The inferior surface of the disc is more closely adapted to the condylar head, especially in its medial and lateral aspects. This constraint promotes rotary movements of the condyle in relation to the disc and glenoid fossa. Anteriorly, inferior reflections of the disc are interspersed with tendinous insertions of the superior head of the lateral pterygoid muscle. Posteriorly, the disc is attached to the inferior lamina of the retrodiscal tissue, which contains elastic fibers and blood vessels (Figure 1.2). As a result of these attachments, rotation takes place in the inferior space, while translation of the joint occurs primarily in the superior joint space. The different movements of the jaw rely upon the contraction of the lateral pterygoid muscle and its angle of attachment to the mandibular condyle (Figure 1.4).

The mouth is capable of opening widely, such as an interincisal opening of greater than 40 mm, as a result of condylar rotation and translation. However, most physiological opening movements are primarily the result of smaller rotations of the condylar head. Under normal conditions, these movements produce complex compressive loads between the anterior surface of the condyle and the posterior slope of the articular eminence [32]. In the presence of a normally positioned disc, forces

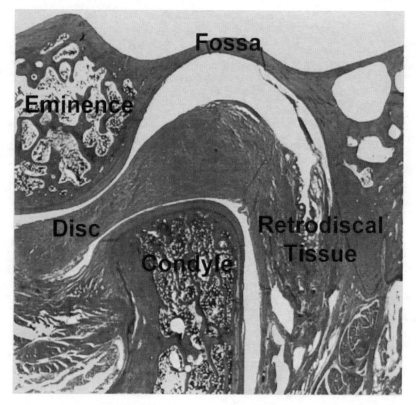

Figure 1.2: Histological sagittal view of the TMJ.

in this region are reduced and dissipated by the interposed intermediate zone of the disc along with the lubricating actions of synovial fluid. The TMJ tissues, particularly the TMJ disc, appear to have been designed to distribute both tensile and compressive forces during jaw movement.

Potential movement of the mandible through three planes of space has already been described. Of interest is the considerably larger bulk of musculature responsible for closing movements as opposed to rotary opening and translatory excursive actions. Closing of the mouth is under the influence of the masseter, temporalis, and medial pterygoid muscles. These muscles form a robust sling around and above the mandible that generate a considerable amount of force. In contrast, opening movements are produced through the relatively small contractions of the lateral pterygoid (Figure 1.4) and (possibly) suprahyoid muscles. This muscular arrangement suggests that under normal conditions opening movements constitute relatively passive actions through smaller ranges, while closing of the mouth invokes a power stroke for chewing.

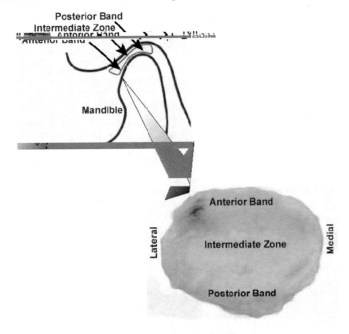

Figure 1.3: TMJ disc in a sagittal and superior view. (Adapted from Wong et al. [28].)

1.3   DEVELOPMENT

A thorough description of the developmental process of the TMJ has been described by Ten Cate in his Oral Histology series of books [33]. Briefly, in the early stages of development, a primary jaw joint is formed by early embryonic cartilage called Meckel's cartilage, named after the anatomist to first describe it. Meckel's cartilage provides the support for the development of the lower jaw and extends from the midline backward and dorsally, and it ends as the malleus. This primary jaw joint exists for about 4 months until the cartilages ossify and become incorporated in the middle ear. At 3 months of gestation, the TMJ begins to form as a secondary and final jaw joint. The first evidence of TMJ development is the appearance of two distinct regions of mesenchymal condensation, the temporal and condylar blastema. The temporal blastema appears before the condylar, and initially both are positioned some distance from each other. The condylar blastema grows rapidly towards the temporal blastema to close the gap. Unlike the long bones, where bone is formed because cartilage ossifies, the TMJ bones are formed from ossification of the blastemas, and then the cartilage is developed. In the TMJ, ossification first begins in the temporal blastema. While the condylar blastema is still condensed mesenchyme, a cleft appears immediately above it that becomes the inferior joint cavity. The condylar blastema differentiates into cartilage, and then a second cleft appears in relation to the temporal ossification that becomes the upper joint cavity. With the appearance of this cleft, the primitive articular disc is formed.

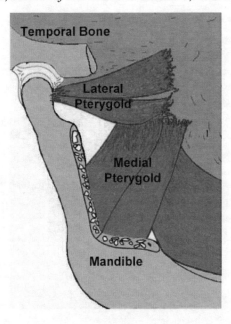

Figure 1.4: Schematic of the musculature surrounding the TMJ. (Adapted from Wong et al. [28].)

1.4   ETIOLOGY, THE TMJ HEALING PROBLEM, AND AGE RELATED CHANGES

It has been reported that up to a quarter of the population have temporomandibular joint disorder (TMD) symptoms [34], but patient studies show that only 3–4% of the population choose to seek treatment [35]. TMJ disorders are characterized by intra-articular positional and/or structural abnormalities. In the 1980s, reports showed prevalence rates ranging from 16% to 59% for symptoms and from 33% to 86% for clinical signs [36], although from 3% to 7% of the adult population has sought care for TMJ pain and dysfunction [37]. Among individuals with TMJ disorders, 11% had symptoms of TMJ osteoarthrosis [38]. It has also been shown that flattening of the condyle and/or eminence was seen in 35% of TMJs in asymptomatic persons [39]. However, once the breakdown in the joint starts, TMJ osteoarthrosis can be crippling, leading to a variety of morphological and functional deformities [40].

The fibrocartilages of the TMJ do not heal after degenerative insults are present. The pathological process is characterized by deterioration and abrasion of articular cartilage and local thickening and remodeling of the underlying bone [40]. These changes are frequently accompanied by the superimposition of secondary inflammatory changes. Therefore, TMJ degeneration can be described as mechanically induced osteoarthrosis, though the term osteoarthritis also seems to be used interchangeably. Internal derangement of the TMJ is defined as an abnormal positional relationship of the disc relative to the mandibular condyle and the articular eminence (Figure 1.5), and it is unclear whether it leads to degeneration or it is caused by degeneration.

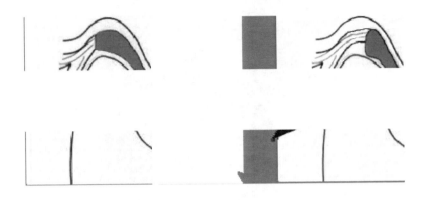

Figure 1.5: Internal derangement (anterior displacement) of the TMJ disc.

Wilkes [41] established five stages based on clinical and imaging criteria to describe internal derangement. A detailed description of these stages can be found in the literature [42]. Briefly, in Stage I clinical observations include painless clicking and unrestricted mandibular motion. When imaged, the disc is displaced slightly forward on opening, although as the disc slides back it produces an audible clicking sound, and the bone contours appear normal. In Stage II, there are complaints of occasional painful clicking, intermittent locking, and headaches. When imaged, the disc appears slightly deformed and displaced, and the bone contours appear normal. In Stage III, there is frequent joint pain and tenderness, headaches, locking, restricted range of mandibular motion, and painful chewing. When imaged, anterior disc displacement is seen, and the disc starts locking on opening. The bony contours remain normal in appearance. In Stage IV, individuals complain of chronic pain, headache, and restricted mandibular range of motion. When imaged, a markedly thickened disc is anteriorly displaced, and abnormal contours to both the condyle and articular eminence begin to become evident. In Stage V, individuals experience pain and crepitus with mandibular function. When imaged, the now grossly deformed disc is anteriorly displaced, and degenerative changes are present in all the bones.

In these later stages of degeneration, removal of the disc and reconstruction of the entire joint using autologous tissue may be required to alleviate pain. However, this treatment does not represent an adequate long-term solution, especially considering the relatively young patient population. The lack of a permanent natural solution for functional repair of the joint results in the need for tissue engineering.

Age is clearly a predisposing factor, because both frequency and severity of the disease appear to increase with aging. For example, the calcium content of the human disc increases progressively with aging [43]. This increase in calcification may be caused by aging or by a changed mechanical stress [44]. Accordingly, the material properties of the disc can also be expected to be related to age [45]. This implies that the disc becomes stiffer and more fragile in nature, reducing its capability to handle overload. Articular cartilages can also change with aging. The molecular weight of hyaluronic acid in human articular cartilage decreases from 2000 to 300 kDa between the ages of 2.5 and 86 yrs [46]. Hyaluronic acid in articular cartilage is essential for it to maintain its viscosity, and any decrease in molecular weight can lead to reduction of its biorheological properties in cartilage.

1.5 PATHOPHYSIOLOGY, CATABOLISM, AND OSTEOARTHROSIS

A well written description of many of the factors associated with the pathophysiology of the TMJ can be found in the literature [42]. Briefly, remodeling is an essential biological response to normal functional demands, ensuring homeostasis of joint form and function, and occlusal relationships [47]. Arnett et al. [48, 49] proposed an explanation for the pathophysiology of the degenerative changes as one that results from dysfunctional articular remodeling due to (1) a decreased adaptive capacity of the articulating structures of the joint or (2) excessive or sustained physical stress to the TMJ articular structures that exceeds the normal adaptive capacity.

A decreased ability of articulating tissues to withstand normal forces maybe be due to many factors affecting the host's general condition such as advancing age, systemic illness, and hormonal factors. These factors may contribute to dysfunctional remodeling of the TMJ, even when the biomechanical stresses are within a normal physiologic range.

Abnormal forces can also be responsible for the degeneration of articulating surfaces, and these forces could be different in magnitude, direction, and time of application. Several events could cause abnormal forces and joint loading such as trauma, parafunction, displaced tissues and/or unstable occlusion [48]–[51]. These factors may occur alone or may be interrelated, interdependent, and/or coexistent. Trauma in the mandible can cause degeneration of the articular cartilage and cause an inflammatory response and produce pain. Trauma has been reported to alter the mechanical properties of the disc [52] and to cause mechanical fatigue of the disc [53, 54]. TMJ alterations have occurred over time after the trauma, leading to progressive condylar resorption and deformation [49].

Parafunction may produce abnormal compression and shear forces capable of initiating disc displacement and condylar and articular eminence degenerative changes [55]. Parafunctional hyper-activity of the lateral pterygoid muscle has been considered to lead to masticatory muscle pain [56, 57]. It has been proposed that dysfunction of the pterygoid muscle can lead to TMJ internal derangement and osteoarthrosis, since the superior head of the lateral pterygoid muscle attaches partly to the articular capsule of the TMJ and directly or indirectly to its articular disc [56, 57].

Mechanical factors can also cause changes in the TMJ structure. Excessive or unbalanced mechanical loading in the TMJ can cause overload of articular tissues, resulting in the onset and progression of TMJ osteoarthrosis. These loading conditions could arise from abnormal/unstable occlusion (how the teeth fit together for bite) and internal derangement of the TMJ disc.

1.6 GUIDELINES FOR TESTING AND MODELING OF TISSUE MECHANICS

A brief summary of mechanical testing modalities and methods for modeling tissue behavior is presented here. Note that this is meant to be a general overview; a more thorough introduction to modeling biomechanical behavior can be found in a book entitled "Introduction to Continuum Biomechanics" authored by Athanasiou and Natoli [58].

Biological tissues have unique characteristics that require more complicated testing methods than those developed for testing of traditional engineering materials. One marked characteristic is the presence of a large water component. Because of this, tests should be performed in a hydrated and osmotically balanced environment similar to what the tissue experiences *in situ*. Most biological tissues also display anisotropic and heterogeneous material properties. Therefore, tests should be performed on multiple regions and in several orientations to illustrate a complete description of a tissue's biomechanical properties.

Most biomechanical experiments performed on cartilaginous tissues can be categorized as either compressive, tensile, shear, or friction tests. In a *compressive* test, the tissue is exposed to either *indentation*, where the force is applied through a small indenter or *confined/unconfined compression*, where a platen is used to compress the entire specimen. It is categorized as either *confined* or *unconfined* depending on whether the tissue is supported or allowed to expand freely on its lateral sides. A test where the sample is pulled is called a *tension* test. This type of test is inherently more complicated and prone to error than a compression test due to the need to grip the sample in some fashion. These tests are classified as either *uniaxial* or *biaxial* depending on whether the sample is pulled along one axis or two axes. A *shear* test is one where a stress is applied parallel to a face of a material. To perform this type of test, a small compressive tare load is applied to a sample situated between two parallel platens. One platen is then translated or rotated parallel to the surface of the sample while recording the load and displacement in that direction. A *friction* test can be performed using a device similar to a shear apparatus, but instead allowing the surfaces to slide against the each other. The *coefficient of friction* is obtained as the ratio of the forces applied parallel and perpendicular to the surface.

A stress-strain curve from a uniaxial tension test is shown in Figure 1.6. In this example, a tissue has been pulled at a constant rate until failure, while measuring force with a load cell. *Stress* is defined as load (force) divided by the sample's cross section, and has units of pressure (force/length^2). *Strain* is a non-dimensional quantity defined as the change in length divided by initial length. An appropriate constitutive model can be fit to a stress-strain curve to obtain material properties. In material mechanics, a constitutive equation is one that relates stress to strain. The most basic model is that of a *linearly elastic solid*, which assumes a linear stress-strain relationship. The *elastic* or *Young's modulus* is defined as the ratio of stress to strain in the range of elastic deformation (the linear region of the curve before the yield point in Figure 1.6), and is a measure of material stiffness. Deformations

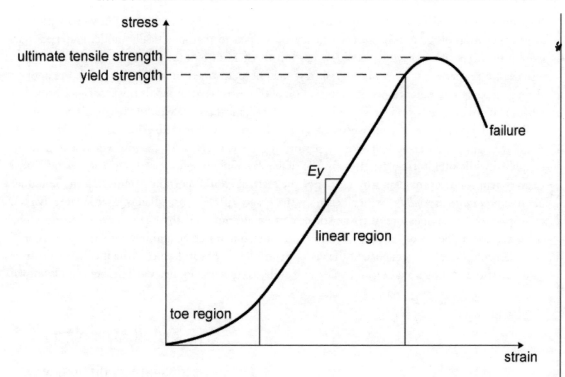

Figure 1.6: Stress vs. strain curve for a tensile test.

that do not exceed the yield point are said to be reversible because the tissue can return to the original shape after the load is released. However, deformations past the yield point are described as plastic as they involve an irreversible change to the underlying tissue structure. The highest stress sustained by a tissue during a test to failure is the *ultimate tensile strength*, and *toughness* is the total area under the curve from zero to maximum strain.

When a tissue is subjected to a tensile strain, there is a resultant contraction in the perpendicular axis. Conversely, compressive strain causes expansion in the transverse dimension. The negative of the ratio of lateral to axial strain is the *Poisson's ratio*, a material property that provides a quantitative measure of compressibility. A material with a Poisson's ratio approaching 0.5 (e.g., rubber) is nearly incompressible. The Poisson's ratio of an anisotropic material, such as the TMJ disc, will vary depending on the region and orientation of loading. Therefore, reported values for the disc have a broad distribution (0 to 0.4) [59, 60].

Though it is widely used, linear elasticity cannot model several important phenomena inherent in soft tissue mechanics. Cartilaginous tissues display time-dependent material properties, e.g., biomechanical properties vary with respect to strain-rate, necessitating the use of methods and models that incorporate this behavior. Two additional phenomena are (1) *creep*: the continued deformation after application of a step load, and (2) *stress relaxation*: the decrease in stress with time after application of a strain. *Viscoelastic theory,* developed to mathematically model materials that exhibit these specific behaviors, is widely used in the field of biomechanics. To examine a tissue's viscoelastic properties, a *creep indentation* test may be performed in which a step load is applied through a porous indenter tip while deformation of the tissue is recorded. If this test is performed in a hydrated environment, and strains are relatively small, most tissues will fully recover after removal of the test load allowing the recovery behavior to be examined as well. Alternatively, a researcher may investigate viscoelastic behavior by performing a *stress relaxation* test, in which a step strain is applied while monitoring the stress in the tissue. By applying an appropriate viscoelastic model (e.g., Kelvin solid) to the data from either of the tests, several important parameters can be found: (1) the *instantaneous modulus*, which describes the tissue stiffness immediately after loading, (2) the *relaxation modulus*, a measure of tissue stiffness at equilibrium, (3) the *coefficient of viscosity*, which describes viscous behavior, and (4) two time constants, one for creep and one for stress relaxation.

An additional consequence of the viscous component of soft tissues is the inequality of stress vs. strain curves during a loading and unloading cycle, as shown in Figure 1.7. This behavior is known

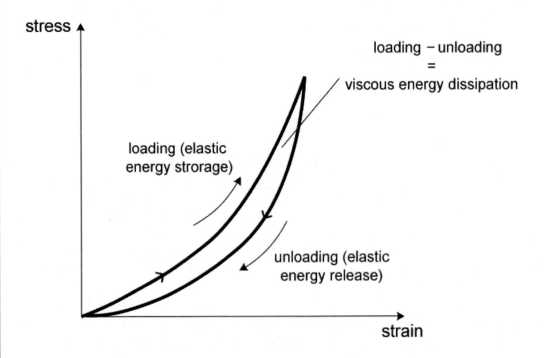

Figure 1.7: Hysteresis for one loading/unloading cycle.

as *hysteresis* and the area between the two curves represents the energy dissipated by the tissue during the cycle. The amount of energy dissipation decreases with repeated application of preconditioning cycles, reaching an equilibrium value after approximately 10 to 15 cycles [61, 62]. As a result, it is important to *precondition* samples prior to testing to minimize sample-to-sample variability due to differences in latent energy storage.

In addition to viscoelasticity, there are other widely-used models that can accurately describe soft tissue mechanics. The *biphasic theory* is a mixture theory specifically developed to describe the deformation of cartilage subjected to a load, though it has been used to describe this behavior in a variety of materials, and is generally preferred over viscoelasticity for compression testing. The biphasic theory assumes the tissue is an immiscible solution consisting of an elastic matrix and a viscous fluid whose viscoelastic effects are the result of drag associated with fluid flow through the matrix. Modeling using biphasic theory gives three material properties: (1) the *aggregate modulus*, which is a measure of tissue stiffness, (2) *permeability*, a measure of the ability of the solid matrix to allow fluid flow, and (3) the *Poisson's ratio*. *Poroelastic theory* is similar to biphasic theory in that it assumes the presence of distinct solid and liquid phases, and with certain assumptions, the two theories are equivalent, though the biphasic theory is derived from basic principles and is not an *ad hoc* theory. A primary tenet of poroelasticity is the principle of effective stress, which states that the total stress in a material is the sum of the stress in its component parts. The *hydraulic permeability* and *Young's modulus* of a material are determined using this model.

TMJ cartilage experiences cyclic loading during mastication, and therefore it is important to describe the dynamic properties of the tissues. If an elastic material such as steel is loaded cyclically, the stress and strain curves will occur in phase. When similar loading is applied to a viscoelastic material, the stress curve will lag behind the strain curve. Two moduli are used to describe dynamic viscoelastic behavior: (1) *storage modulus*, the in-phase stress to strain ratio, which describes elastic energy storage, and (2) *loss modulus*, the out-of-phase stress to strain ratio, which is a measure of viscous energy dissipation. The vector sum of these moduli, known as the *dynamic (or complex) modulus*, is often reported. The storage modulus represents the real part of the complex modulus, and the loss modulus represents the imaginary part. The ratio of the loss to the storage moduli is the loss tangent, which is a measure of the viscous damping of a material (e.g., the loss tangent is zero for a perfectly elastic material). Dynamic tests under compression, tension and shear have been performed for both the TMJ disc and the mandibular condyle [63]–[71].

1.7   THE BIOMECHANICAL ENVIRONMENT OF THE TMJ

It is important for the tissue engineer to have a thorough understanding of the biomechanical environment of the TMJ, and the combination forces the tissues experience *in situ*. A description of the native physiological environment can be used to design novel bioreactors, which enhance engineered construct properties through activation of mechanotransductive signaling pathways. Additionally, an understanding of joint forces and motions provide insight into the etiology of tissue degradation.

Hylander [72]–[74] brought an interest to quantifying *in vivo* strains in the TMJ, and both compressive and tensile strains have been observed [75]–[77], with bone strains ranging from 89 to 109 $\mu\varepsilon$ (microstrain) during masseter contraction in miniature pigs [78]. In terms of condyle loading, axial compressive loads on the condyle of up to approximately 32 N in baboons were calculated in bite-force experiments [79], and forces up to 210 N were reported on human condyles under simulated muscle activity. Investigators have also measured hydrostatic pressure of the TMJ to further elucidate the biomechanical environment [80]–[82], revealing negative pressures at rest or upon opening [80, 82] and pressures up to 200 mmHg (27 kPa) during clenching [82].

The TMJ disc is subjected to complex combinations of tensile, compressive, and shear loads during mastication [83]–[86]. The surfaces of the mandibular condyle and temporal bone are incongruent and consequently impart non-uniform loads across the surface of the disc during rotating and translating motions. During chewing motions, the contact angles between the TMJ articulating surfaces change due to the presence of a bolus of food between the teeth. Additionally, the two TMJs are bilateral and not capable of moving independently of the contralateral side. These factors conspire to make the task of modeling disc loading and behavior a highly intricate undertaking. Nevertheless, many 3-D reconstructions of joint motions have been made using combinations of advanced imaging techniques, finite element models, and appropriate material models. As a result, these studies are essential for understanding the biomechanical environment of the disc.

Early finite element studies modeled the disc in two dimensions [87, 88]. Chen and Xu [87] investigated disc displacement and stress distribution by modeling sagittal condylar motions. They recorded tensile forces along the superior surface of the intermediate zone while compressive forces were located at the upper and lower boundaries of the posterior band. A maximum compressive stress of 12 MPa was recorded at the lower boundary of the posterior band. DeVocht et al. [89] performed a similar analysis and were able to simulate normal disc movement within the joint without the need for peripheral attachments. Beek et al. [85] created a 3-D finite element model of the TMJ disc from a mature adult donor post-mortem using a magnetic tracking device to investigate load distribution in the disc during simulated clenching. The simulation yielded large deformations in the intermediate zone relative to other regions (maximum of 0.44 strain) and relatively large von Mises stress concentrations (2.79 MPa) in the lateral region (von Mises stress is a scalar value calculated from a 3-D stress tensor that is often presented in finite element analysis results; it is indicative of the general state of stress). Tanaka et al. [86] created individual-specific, 3-D finite element models of subjects with or without disc displacement using magnetic resonance images (MRI) taken during mandibular motion. Models from volunteers without derangement showed high stresses in the anterior and lateral regions of the disc during jaw opening while symptomatic subjects showed greater stress in the posterior connective tissues. The maximum recorded von Mises stresses were approximately 5 MPa. Additionally, the calculated frictional coefficients were 0.001 for asymptomatic volunteers, and 0.01 - 0.001 for patients with internal derangement.

While these early studies assumed the disc to behave as a linearly elastic solid, more physiologically accurate material models have been implemented to describe finite deformations and inhomogeneous load distributions in the disc. Chen et al. [90] implemented a hyperelastic model and demonstrated high compressive stresses in the posterior band and high tensile stresses on the superior surface. Beek et al. [91] found that the disc can effectively be modeled as a poroelastic material as long as the solid structure is assumed to be hyperelastic. More recently, Pérez del Palomar and Doblaré [92] implemented a fiber-reinforced porohyperelastic model, which takes into account the disc's collagen fiber orientation to model behavior under clenching forces. The results of this study demonstrate that finite element models that assume an isotropic disc tend to overestimate forces in the intermediate zone and underestimate stresses in the peripheral areas and in the pore fluid.

In a 2005 review [93], Gallo described the use of a six-axis mandibular tracking device in combination with MRI to obtain a non-invasive model of intra-articular TMJ dynamics, a technique referred to as dynamic stereometry [94]. The group has used this technology in several studies to report some interesting results. First, both TMJs are loaded during chewing, the balancing side actually more so than the working side [32, 95]. Second, while performing chewing motions at 1 Hz, a 2.1 MPa stress-field was shown to move mediolaterally across the disc during opening and lateromedially during closing in healthy volunteers [32, 96]. The work done during these motions was estimated as high as 700 mJ, potentially causing fatigue in the disc after long-term exposure. Lastly, they noted higher mechanical energy density in the lateral region of the disc [32], corroborating the findings of other researchers and providing a plausible explanation for the high incidence of tears in this region [41, 92].

1.8   ANIMAL MODELS

In vitro tissue engineering efforts begin and end with the crucial choice of an animal model. As discussed previously, characterization work is initially performed on several animals to elucidate the intrinsic similarities and differences between them and the patient population. Here, the most similar model is selected and its characteristics are used as design criteria. The next step after *in vitro* work is to test the ability of the constructs to withstand the *in vivo* environment. Typically, a large and a small animal model are chosen. Though large animals such as pigs, goats, cows, and primates have more anatomical similarities to the human, it is usually not feasible nor is it ethically responsible to perform initial evaluations in large animals; therefore, initial *in vivo* work should be performed in a small model.

For cartilaginous tissues, preliminary *in vivo* testing in a small animal model usually involves the use of immunocompromised mice. Indeed, subcutaneous implantation in nude mice has been used extensively as a preliminary *in vivo* evaluation for tissue engineered cartilage [97]–[106] and fibrocartilages including meniscus [107]–[109] and intervertebral disc [110]–[112]. The goal of such studies is to examine the ability of constructs to remain viable and maintain characteristics imparted during *in vitro* culture. Of course, this environment would not recapitulate the forces and biochemical signals present in the joint; therefore, further study would be necessary in a larger animal model. The smallest and most likely animal model to evaluate the performance of a tissue engineered construct is the rabbit. Rabbits are commonly used for orthopedic joint defect studies, and there is a precedent for use of rabbits for mandibular condyle defects [113]–[119].

Beyond the rabbit, several factors are important to consider for selection of a large animal model for TMJ reconstruction. May and Saha [120] listed these as (1) similarity to the human TMJ,

(2) cost, (3) subject pool size, (4) availability, and (5) ethical acceptance. Factors to include when evaluating similarity are disc morphology, joint anatomy, masticatory patterns, and biochemical and biomechanical characteristics. The porcine model has been identified as the most similar non-primate to the human, and therefore the most appropriate large animal for biomechanical and tissue engineering studies [121]–[124]. Bermejo et al. [124] noted morphological similarities such as disc size and shape, anatomical similarities of the respective joints, similar masticatory patterns, and that pigs are omnivorous. Other species examined as models included cows [125, 126], dogs [127, 128], goats [129], rabbits [130, 131], rats [132, 133], and sheep [134, 135]. It is important to understand that no model will be identical to the human. In the pig, the retrodiscal tissue is fibrous while in the human it is vascular, and the zygomatic process in pigs is extended further inferiorly over the lateral aspect of the condyle than in humans [136]. Some minor differences also exist in the structure of the masticatory musculature [137]. These differences are relatively minor when compared to the disparity in size, structure, and masticatory patterns between humans and other non-primate animal models.

1.9   CURRENT THERAPIES

Eventually the patient will seek treatment for any of the symptoms of TMDs described earlier. At this stage the clinician will have several choices of treatments depending on the particular pathology and the stage of pain or degeneration. At early stages, non-invasive treatments are always recommended to try to correct the problem. Once non-invasive treatments are not effective, then clinicians turn to minimally invasive procedures to try to free up adhesions, wash debris, and reposition tissues. However, when both treatment modalities fail, surgeons may embark on removing damaged tissues (disc, condyle), and even perform a total joint replacement. This section explains these treatment modalities in further detail, but a thorough review can be found in the literature [42].

1.9.1   NON-INVASIVE TREATMENTS

Commonly used non-invasive treatments for TMDs include occlusal splint, medications, orthotics, and physical therapy. In the clinic, occlusal splints are the most common treatment for TMJ pain. In a controlled study on the effects of occlusal splint therapy, a reduction of clinical signs was seen in individuals with severe TMJ degeneration [138]. However, there is a lack of evidence to the effectiveness of splint therapy in relieving pain when compared with that of general pain treatment methods [139]. In terms of medications, muscle relaxants may be helpful in controlling the reflex masticatory muscle spasm/pain [140]. Oral orthotics, can often aid in the control of parafunctional behaviors and provide relief from masticatory muscle spasm/pain, which along with a soft diet, could decrease the stresses experienced in the TMJ. Other examples of non-invasive treatments would include superficial warm and moist heat or localized cold to facilitate joint mobilization, or therapeutic exercises to increase muscle strength and retain a functional range of motion. Ultrasound, electrogalvanic stimulation, and massage techniques also seem to be helpful in reducing inflammation and pain [141].

1.9.2   MINIMALLY INVASIVE TREATMENTS

Arthrocentesis is a minimally invasive procedure where the surgeon will use a sterile needle to drain fluid from the joint, and then flush the joint with a sterile solution to lubricate the joint surfaces and reduce inflammation [142]. TMJ arthroscopy, while less invasive than open surgery, is more invasive than arthrocentesis. However, arthroscopy may be especially valuable in terms of early diagnosis and management of TMJ disorders, particularly early stage arthritis [143]. Unfortunately, some disorders such as late stage ankylosis or fibrosis can make it extremely difficult to perform arthroscopy. While the majority of persons with TMJ osteoarthrosis can be adequately managed with non-invasive/minimally invasive procedures, there is a small percentage of these patients (< 20%) who are considered for surgery [144].

1.9.3   TMJ SURGICAL THERAPIES

Although reshaping of articular surfaces may help to mitigate symptoms of TMJ disorders, various limitations to this approach led to approaches including the transplantation of autologous tissues and implantation of alloplastic materials. Several different autologous tissues have been advocated as a replacement for the TMJ disc [145]; however, one of the most popular procedures is the use of the vascularized local temporalis muscle flap [146].

Pre-existing disorders of the TMJ such as internal derangement, progressive condylar resorption, osteoarthrosis, condylar hyperplasia, osteochondroma, congenital deformities, and non-salvageable joints may reduce the success of surgical outcomes [147]. The resultant pathology may result in a compromised foundation for reconstruction of the maxillofacial skeletal structure, especially in conditions where there are gross erosive changes in the articulating components of both the fossa and condyle. Moreover, the degenerative changes associated with these conditions make the affected components of the TMJ highly susceptible to failure under the new functional loading resulting from surgical repositioning of the maxillofacial skeletal structures.

1.9.4   INVASIVE SURGICAL THERAPIES – TOTAL JOINT REPLACEMENT

The costochondral graft is the autologous structure most frequently recommended for the TMJ reconstruction [148]. However, orthopedists recommend alloplastic reconstruction when total joint replacement is required for the management of a patient (of sufficient skeletal maturity) with joint degeneration [149]. In the TMJ, alloplastic reconstruction has been discussed at length [150]–[155]. It is generally agreed that when the mandibular condyle is extensively damaged, degenerated, or lost, as in arthritic conditions, replacement with either autologous graft or alloplastic implant is an acceptable approach to achieve optimal functional improvement and return to a functional state [144], [156]–[158].

1.10   TMJ REPAIR USING ALLOPLASTIC DEVICES

There are many published studies on the use of alloplastic devices for TMJ repair, focusing on the whole spectrum from design and validation of the device, catastrophic outcomes, to long-term successful management of patients with severe TMDs. The following section recaps the description of the history and current use of alloplastic devices found in the book chapter of Wong et al. in Tissue Engineering and Artificial Organs [28].

1.10.1   PAST EXPERIENCES

Experiences with different alloplastic materials for TMJ disc replacement have been characterized by a number of significant failures resulting in severe joint resorption, alteration of mandibular skeletal relationships, compromised motion, pain, and even systemic immune compromise. These surgical disasters and the resultant lawsuits have unfortunately tainted all forms of TMJ surgery and discouraged many surgeons from seeking alternative methods to reconstruct the joint. Before the controversy surrounding the implantation of medical-grade silicone, interpositional implants (silastic) were available for disc replacement. As permanent replacements, these devices were prone to fragmentation, but when used as a temporary interpositional implant ("pull-out" technique), they were observed to provoke the formation of a dense fibrous tissue capsule, which served as an interarticular cushion. Their relatively successful use following discectomy might be attributed to this reaction.

One of the alloplastic replacements of a disc with the most litigation occurred with the use of a Teflon–Proplast implant in the late 1980s and early 1990s. Produced by the Vitek Corporation, fragmentation of the implant under functional and parafunctional loads was associated with an exuberant foreign body giant cell response and significant osteoclastic activity, resulting in the resorption of condylar and fossa surfaces and severe local inflammatory events. Despite the immense suffering experienced by the patients who were unfortunate enough to be treated with this implant, the lessons learned from this experience are essential, and include the significance of characterizing the loading patterns within a joint, and the importance of recognizing the effects of degradation products upon the local joint environment.

1.10.2   CURRENTLY APPROVED THERAPIES

The TMJ hemi-arthroplasty was a procedure popularized by Christensen and Morgan in the 1960s, in which the superior articulation of the joint was replaced with an implant fabricated out of chrome–cobalt alloy. The Christensen implant reconstructed both the fossa and articular eminence while the Morgan implant covered the eminence only. Concerns over accelerated degeneration of the natural condyle articulating against a less-deformable surface eventually resulted in the replacement of the hemi-arthroplasty with total joint reconstructive procedures utilizing both prosthetic fossa and condylar components. Currently, three total joint replacement systems are licensed by the Food and Drug Administration (FDA) for implantation into patients, though limitations have been imposed on surgeons wishing to use these devices and the selection of patient candidates. Stringent follow-up of patients treated with these implants form the basis of various clinical trials designed to test not only the ability of the procedure to improve a patient's condition, but also the integrity of the devices over time.

Customization of alloplastic implants: The ability to customize an alloplastic device is also useful for correcting a skeletal discrepancy that may occur in patients with severe degenerative joint disease, where retrusion and rotation of the mandible is the result of decreased posterior vertical support (Figure 1.8). Customized prosthetic devices involve complex surgical techniques. In order to accu-

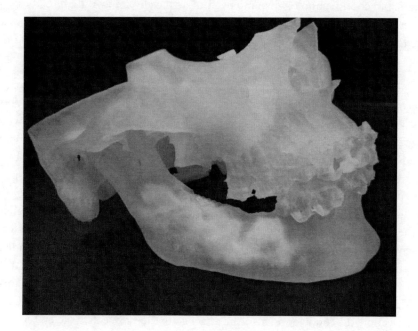

Figure 1.8: Rapid prototype of skull obtained from computer tomography (CT) scans.

rately reproduce the skeletal bases to which the devices will be attached, two separate surgeries are ideally required. During the first procedure, the diseased joint (or failed implant) is removed and the area debrided. A temporary alloplastic space maintaining implant is used to reduce the amount of soft tissue in-growth into the resulting space. Following this surgery, a thin-cut computerized tomography (CT) scan is obtained using a protocol devised by companies specializing in the fabrication of stereolithographic models. The anatomically accurate model is sent to a joint fabrication company where CAD–CAM technology is used to produce a prototype of the final device. Each device is composed of a prosthetic fossa and eminence as well as a condylar head attached to a ramus component. The prototype is returned to the surgeon who confirms that the surgical defect has been correctly reconstructed.

At this time, minor modifications to the skeletal defect may be proposed to better accommodate and fit the implant. Once the customized implant has been completed, the patient undergoes a second surgery during which the surgical sites are adjusted to match the defect created on the stereolithographic model before the prosthetic fossa and condyle are attached to their bony bases.

The entire process is time-consuming and expensive, but justification for its use lies in the magnitude of the problem requiring correction.

Single surgery reconstruction of a joint is also possible with custom devices. In this procedure, a stereolithographic model of the diseased joint is prepared. If an alloplastic device is already in place, digital subtraction technology is employed to artificially remove the prosthesis. Otherwise, the surgeon creates the anticipated surgical defect on the model and the device is fabricated. Minor adjustments to the skeletal remnants can be made at the time of implantation to promote a close adaptation of the device to the defect.

Available implants: The Christensen total joint system has been available since 1965, though the current device, which employs a vitallium fossa articulating against a chrome–cobalt condylar head, is significantly modified from the original design, which used a metallic fossa matched with a condylar head composed of polymethylmethacrylate (PMMA). Concerns over the development of a giant cell mediated foreign body response to particulate PMMA prompted this change. Both the fossa and condylar prosthesis are fixated to the temporal bone and mandibular ramus, respectively, with screws. Both patient-specific implants, customized according to computerized tomographic data, as well as stock devices with different sizes and shapes for the fossa and condyle are available.

Another system currently available is offered by TMJ Concepts. This system utilizes a chromium–cobalt–molybdenum condylar head attached to a ramus framework made out of titanium alloy (6AL–4V) and a fossa component composed of ultra-high molecular weight polyethylene (UHMWPE) with a non-alloy titanium mesh backing. The respective components are customized to the individual patient's anatomical defect and are produced with advanced CAD–CAM technology. After fabrication, the condyle and fossa are attached to their respective skeletal components with multiple screws (titanium alloy) placed in a nonlinear fashion to promote maximum stability. This system has been followed by Mercuri and coworkers to determine its long-term outcome [158, 159]. The authors determined that indeed the prosthetic proved to be a safe and effective long-term management modality. This was based on 30% improvement in mandibular motion and a 76% reduction in pain scores after 10 years, along with 85% reported quality of life scores that showed improvement since baseline after 14 years. Further, Mercuri et al. [157] observed that multiply operated patients previously exposed to failed Proplast-Teflon alone or both failed Proplast-Teflon and silastic have poorer reported long-term outcomes than ones implanted with the TMJ Concepts prosthetic.

The third device with FDA approval is the Biomet Microfixation prosthetic total joint. The fossa consists of a UHMWPE articular surface mounted on a metallic base which is used to secure the prosthesis with screws to the lateral margins of the glenoid fossa. Since this is a stock device available in three sizes, the patient's anatomy requires preparation to conform to the prosthetic contours. This is achieved in part by removing most of the articular eminence and if indicated, filling the space between the fossa and device with orthopedic cement (e.g., Simplex P). A significant difference between the design of this fossa prosthesis and those used in the Christensen or TMJ Concepts systems is the thickness of the articular surface. The Biomet total joint system attempts to shift the center of rotation of the reconstructed joint inferiorly to simulate translatory movements by increasing the thickness of the UHMWPE. The condylar portion of this device is composed of a cobalt–chromium–molybdenum alloy.

1.11   IMMUNE RESPONSE, IMMUNOGENICITY, TRANSPLANTS

As tissue engineering of TMJ structures progresses, careful consideration must be given to the potential immune response that these implants will elicit. Until then, it is best to learn from the field of cartilage transplantation. A review of the immune response of cartilage transplants can be found in the literature [160]. Briefly, cartilage lesions which do not penetrate the underlying subchondral bone are unable to self-repair spontaneously. However, full-thickness defects have been shown to undergo only a transient healing response, producing tissue of poor quality that resorbs quickly [161, 162]. Analogously, some researchers believe cartilage lesions less than 3 mm in diameter self-repair with hyaline-like cartilage [163]–[166]. In contrast, it is widely accepted that larger defects are replaced with fibrous cartilage possessing different structure and composition compared to normal cartilage with accompanying inferior mechanical properties [167, 168].

Numerous strategies have been employed to repair cartilage defects with an end goal of filling the defect with tissue having biochemical and biomechanical properties approximating the surrounding native tissue. Such clinical and experimental efforts include subchondral drilling (e.g., microfracture technique) [169], osteochondral graft transplantation [170]– [175], suspended chondrocyte implantation [176, 177], and tissue engineered grafting [178]–[180]. A number of studies have investigated these treatment options and varying degrees of efficacy and immune responses in clinical trials and *in vivo* animal experiments have been reported. Though several methodological variations may be attributed to these differences, controversy and uncertainty remain with respect to the best available treatment option.

Organ transplantation has been investigated extensively, yet the process by which rejection occurs is only moderately understood. Traditionally, transplantation of a graft from a genetically-different donor causes an acute immune response in the host due to the detection of foreign cells [181, 182]. This detection sets in motion a series of cascade events that eventually lead to graft rejection. The first phase of rejection includes the recognition and sensitization phase, whereby T lymphocytes (both positive for the cell surface antigens/markers CD4 and CD8) recognize alloantigen (foreign protein) and respond immediately by undergoing proliferation and activation. Simultaneously, a population of leukocytes migrates from the graft tissue to the host's lymphoid organs whereby they stimulate the host's immune system. During migration, these passenger leukocytes undergo maturation from immature dendritic cells to mature antigen presenting cells (APCs) that activate an array of T lymphocytes, including CD4+, CD8+ [183]. Thus, activation occurs through the interaction of the host T cell with an APC from the donor graft that expresses an appropriate antigenic ligand on its major histocompatibility complex (MHC) receptor [184].

The second phase of immune rejection, known as the effector stage, occurs when the proliferation and activation of T lymphocytes activate other pathways. Activated T cells secrete various cytokines, which rapidly enhance the immune system's response by recruiting a variety of other host immune cells and inducing increased expression of MHC class I and class II molecules of cells from the donor graft [181]–[184]. IL-2 is also critical in the generation of cytotoxic T lymphocytes which attack APCs, while IFN-γ also promotes the influx of macrophages into the graft and their later destructive activation. Finally, TNF-β has a direct, cytotoxic effect on graft cells.

Articular cartilage's avascularity has led to an assertion that the tissue is immuno-privileged, whereby a body's immune system is limited in its ability to detect and reject implanted tissue. However, many researchers have shown that both chondrocytes and their embedded extracellular matrix (ECM) contain antigens that can be immunogenic [185, 186]. Chondrocytes have been found to contain MHC class II antigens, which during transplantation could react with T-cells and elicit a cell-mediated immune response as described above [177, 187]. Additionally, chondrocytes are known to be susceptible to attack by natural killer cells [188]–[190], and various components of the matrix itself have been shown to have antigenic properties including collagens type II, IX, and XI and proteoglycan core proteins [191]–[195]. However, when cartilage tissue is intact, chondrocytes are protected and separated from contact with both natural killer and T-cells by the ECM, which is believed to impart the immuno-privileged nature of intact cartilage [185].

1.12   GENDER PARADOX

It is widely known that more women than men are treated for TMD. Reports of the female-to-male patient prevalence vary from 3:1 to 8:1 [34, 196]. As reviewed by Warren and Fried [197], pain onset in TMD patients is most prevalent in women aged 20 to 40 years. In contrast to patient populations, Gray et al. [35] report that epidemiologic surveys show that the numbers of men and women with TMDs in the general population are roughly equal. However, other studies have found that about 10% to 15% more women than men experience signs and symptoms [34, 198]. For examples, in a 2005 survey of Swedish adolescents, twice as many girls reported TMJ pain when compared to boys [199]. Further, a U.S. adult national health interview survey in 2008 observed that 6.3% of females surveyed reported temporomandibular joint and muscle disorders, while only 2.8% of men reported problems [200].

If there is truly a significant difference between the number of men and women affected by TMDs, then it is possible that this difference can be attributed to reactions of tissues to hormones. In baboons, estrogen receptors were found in the TMJ complex of females but not of males [201, 202]. In addition, a larger number of estrogen-positive and progesterone-positive receptors were found in discs of TMD patients than in normal discs [203]. In contrast, the results of another study propose that the presence of estrogen receptors does not contribute to TMDs in humans [196].

However, more recent thinking suggests that it is possible that female sex hormones play a role in pain transmission [204, 205], and because pain is the most common reason for seeking treatment, women may therefore be more likely to seek treatment. Bragdon et al. [206] in 2002 published a study comparing the threshold to pain of women with TMD to pain free women and men in the presence of opioids. The authors noted that female TMD patients appear unable to effectively engage normal pain-inhibitory systems, probably because of opioid desensitization and/or downregulation. A study used Fos-like immunoreactivity (Fos-LI) to quantify the pattern and magnitude of neural activation within the trigeminal brainstem complex of male and female rats caused by acute inflammatory injury to the TMJ to assess pain [207]. The authors found that morphine caused a greater dose-related reduction in Fos-LI in males than females. Gold and coworkers [208]–[212] have performed a significant amount of work to elucidate pain transmission in the TMJ. In one study, in which they examined the effects of hormones on TMJ pain, they retrogradely labeled TMJ neurons from ovariectomized rats and ovariectomized rats receiving chronic estrogen replacement, three days after injecting the TMJ with either saline or Complete Freund's Adjuvant to induce inflammation [212]. Excitability was assessed with depolarizing current injection to determine action potential threshold. The authors observed that the effects were additive with neurons from rats receiving both estrogen and inflammation. They inferred that the influence of estrogen on both baseline and inflammation-induced changes in TMJ neuronal excitability may help explain the profound sex difference observed in TMD as well as suggest a novel target for the treatment of this pain condition.

CHAPTER 2

Fibrocartilage of the TMJ Disc

2.1 INTRODUCTION

The temporomandibular joint (TMJ) disc (also intra-articular disc or TMJ meniscus) is a unique structure that allows for normal jaw movement and concomitant functions, including the ability to eat and talk. The disc is often mistakenly assumed to be functionally and structurally equivalent to the better-characterized hyaline articular cartilage that covers the end surfaces of long bones and the fibrocartilaginous menisci of the knee joint. In the following sections, similarities and differences among these tissues will be highlighted to provide the tissue engineer a complete set of design criteria which will be valuable when working to design and create a successful engineered disc. Particular attention will be paid to connections linking mechanical function and behavior to underlying disc structure.

2.2 ANATOMY: STRUCTURE AND ATTACHMENTS

The articulating disc of the human TMJ is a biconcave, elliptical, fibrocartilaginous tissue situated between the mandibular condyle and the glenoid fossa. Because of its position, it effectively divides the joint into superior and inferior spaces, as noted in Chapter 1. From a superior view (Figure 2.1), it appears as an ellipse, longer in the mediolateral direction than the anteroposterior direction, and measuring approximately 19 by 13 mm in humans. The disc can be roughly divided into three topographical zones: the posterior band, the intermediate zone, and the anterior band. When viewed in a sagittal section (Figure 2.1), it is clear that the anterior and posterior bands of the disc are much thicker than the intermediate zone. The posterior band is the thickest region, measuring approximately 4 mm. The anterior band is slightly thinner than the posterior, and the intermediate zone is the thinnest region, approximately 1 mm. This shape imparts some important functional characteristics to the disc. The intermediate zone fills the void space between the two joint surfaces when the jaw is occluded, separating and protecting these two incongruent surfaces [Figure 2.2(a)]. During mastication, the intermediate zone imparts some flexibility to the disc, allowing smooth and coordinated movement amid the complex rotational and translatory action present within the joint [Figure 2.2(b)]. On the other hand, the thicker peripheral bands help to maintain disc positioning and structure, thereby preventing internal derangement.

The TMJ disc is attached along its entire periphery to both the condyle and the temporal bone through a complex network of fibrous connective tissues that form a synovial capsule that envelops the joint (Figures 2.3 and 2.4). The rear of the disc blends with a loose network of vascular, fibro-elastic tissue called the bilaminar zone, which is attached to the posterior wall of the glenoid fossa superiorly, and the base of the condyle inferiorly. The anterior end of the disc is attached to

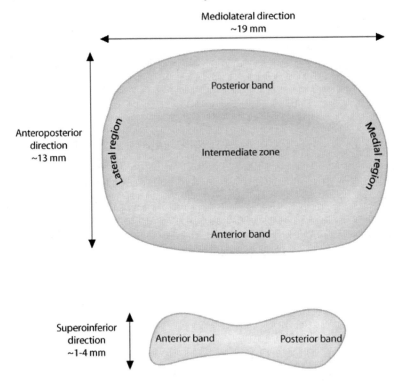

Figure 2.1: Schematic representation of the regions of the human disc in superior (top) and sagittal views, approximating the native dimensions and topography.

the articular eminence of the temporal bone and the anterior horn of the condyle at a depression called the pterygoid fovea. On the medial and lateral sides, the disc merges with the capsule and in turn attaches to the medial and lateral sides of the condylar neck. Generally, speaking, the superior surface of the disc translates with respect to the glenoid fossa. In contrast, the inferior surface of the disc, closely matched to the round contours of the condylar head, experiences mainly rotational movements.

2.3   BIOCHEMICAL CONTENT

Aside from the water content, which constitutes between 66 and 80% of the disc's weight [213], the primary extracellular matrix (ECM) component of the TMJ disc is collagen type I. This marks an important distinction between the fibrocartilage of the disc and hyaline articular cartilage, which is primarily collagen type II, and also the fibrocartilage of the knee meniscus, which contains substantial type I and II components. In addition to collagen, the other major ECM components in the disc

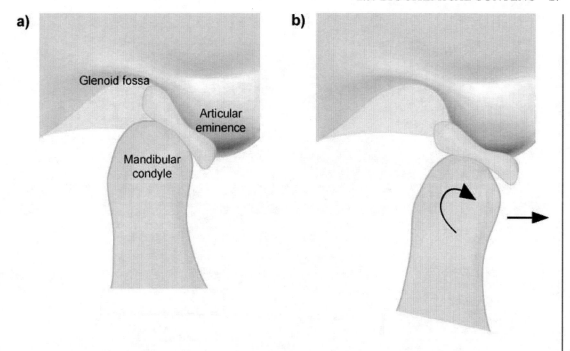

Figure 2.2: Location of the disc relative to the joint surfaces (a) with jaw occlusion and (b) movement of the disc with mandibular motion.

are elastic fibers, glycosaminoglycans, and proteoglycans. These components, and their regional distribution and organization, are covered in detail in the following subsections.

2.3.1   COLLAGEN COMPOSITION AND DISTRIBUTION

A dense network of collagen fibers defines the architecture of the TMJ disc. This ubiquitous protein, present in nearly all connective tissues, is responsible for the majority of the disc's mechanical behaviors. Overall, collagen constitutes approximately 30% of the wet weight [214], 83-96% of the dry weight [215, 216] and 55% of the total volume [217]. Regional variation in collagen concentration is contradictory. Mills et al. [218] reported higher concentrations in the posterior and anterior bands than in the center of the rat disc, but later Almarza et al. [216] reported the opposite in porcine discs. In both cases, however, the reported differences were small. As mentioned previously, the overwhelming majority of collagen in the disc is type I, although the presence of other types has been reported. Collagen type II, the primary fibrilar collagen present in hyaline cartilage, has been found localized around disc cells using immunohistochemistry [218] and later detected in digested discs with Western blot analyses [219]. Detamore et al. [220] observed only faint collagen type II staining in the posterior and anterior bands of the porcine disc via immunohistochemical staining, while large clusters of collagen II were found separating dense bands of collagen type I throughout

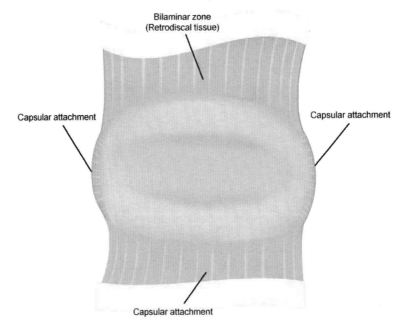

Figure 2.3: Superior view of the disc showing peripheral attachments.

the intermediate zone. Type III collagen is a fibrilar cartilage most notably associated with skin, blood vessels, and granulation tissue, and some research suggests at least trace amounts are present in the TMJ disc at early developmental stages [221] and in newly formed tissue [222]. However, neither Landesberg et al. [219] nor Gage et al. [214] detected collagen type III in bovine or human discs, respectively.

Non-fibrilar collagen types VI, IX, and XII have also been identified in small quantities in bovine and rabbit discs [219, 223]. Collagen Type VI is known to be present in larger quantities in immature articular cartilage and also localized in the pericellular matrix of mature chondrocytes. Collagen types IX and XII form molecular bridges between adjacent type II and type I fibers, respectively, and there is some evidence that they also bind GAG chains of small dermatan sulfate proteoglycans. In light of these findings, more research into the origins of the various collagens and their potential role in development and function in the disc is warranted. For simplicity, however, the collagen of the disc is mostly type I with type II in relatively small amounts found in the intermediate zone. Researchers should make use of this distinction when evaluating the similarities between tissue engineered constructs and the native disc.

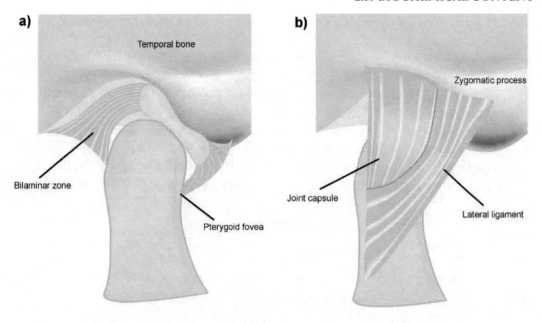

Figure 2.4: Sagittal view of the disc with attachments (a), and with the joint capsule and the lateral ligament (b).

2.3.2   COLLAGEN ORGANIZATION

The orientation of collagen contributes greatly to a tissue's mechanical behavior, and scanning electron microscopy (SEM) studies have revealed considerable information about the organization of collagen in the disc. In a study of the TMJ disc of rhesus monkeys, Taguchi et al. [224] described a thinly woven network of collagen fibers superficially on the disc, anteroposteriorly oriented fibers deeper in the intermediate zone, and dense fibers around the periphery encircling the central region. In another SEM study, Minarelli et al. [225] examined healthy human discs from fetal to mature adult donors, noting that collagen was arranged in compact bundles. In the posterior region, collagen formed thick bundles arranged in a ring which continued around the periphery of the disc and into the anterior region where they blended with bundles of anteroposteriorly and obliquely oriented fibers. Detamore et al. [220] corroborated several of these findings in a more recent study of the porcine disc, noting a ring of collagen fibers around the periphery, with some branching in the posterior band and considerable branching in the anterior band. Mills et al. [218] used polarized light to examine the organization of collagen in primate discs, noting the presence of two distinct regions. In the posterior and anterior bands, fibers were primarily oriented mediolaterally with additional fibers traveling obliquely through the center of these zones. In the intermediate band, the fibers were oriented sagittally with a noticeably greater density and crimping than in the outer bands. Fibers arched to form connections in the areas between these zones. Scapino et al. [226] examined coronal sections of a human disc with a polarized light microscope and discovered thick vertical bundles in the anterior and posterior bands. Many fibers branched diagonally joining the horizontal fibers of the intermediate zone, while some fibers were seen spanning the entire thickness before turning transversely at the surfaces.

Consistent findings from these studies and others [131], [227]–[229] can be summarized as follows: The fibers display a characteristic crimping pattern throughout with a reported mean periodicity between 8 and 23 μm [131, 214, 224, 230, 231]. Thick bands of fibers are assembled in a ring-like structure around the periphery of the disc. In the anterior and posterior bands, the fibers run mediolaterally (Figure 2.5). Conversely, in the medial and lateral regions the fibers align

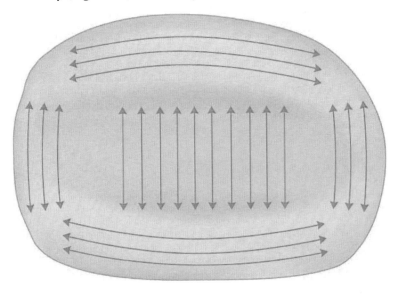

Figure 2.5: The disc with arrows representing the predominant collagen orientation.

anteroposteriorly. Fibers in the intermediate zone align prominently in the anteroposterior direction, though mediolateral and oblique fibers are present in smaller numbers. In the boundaries between these regions, transitional fibers are found bridging the discordant groupings. Covering the upper and lower surfaces of the disc is a thin layer of undulating fibers with foveae of varying diameter. Taken as a whole, these observations suggest certain aspects of functionality in the disc. The undulating collagen fibers may impart relative compliance to the disc at low strains, thereby allowing it to conform more readily to the incongruencies of the joint surfaces. The anteroposteriorly oriented fibers suggest tensile loading occurs mostly in this direction. The thick peripheral bands probably help to maintain the shape of the disc during loading and also help to restore the initial shape upon removal of loads. This collagen ring is reminiscent of the radial bands of collagen in the knee meniscus. There, the bands constrain the lateral displacement during compressive loading through development of tensile hoop stresses. The analogous fibers in the disc may function in a similar way, constraining lateral deformation during compressive loading [131]. Lastly, the thin foveae present on the disc surfaces allow for storage and diffusion of synovial fluid, effectively reducing friction.

2.3.3   ELASTIN

The presence of elastin in the TMJ disc has been described in many studies [218, 220], [232]–[237]. Elastic fibers are found throughout the disc in small numbers making up between 1-2% of the tissue mass [235]. In contrast to elastin found in the ear or nose, which forms large bundles, the elastin in the disc exists as intermittent fibers with a relatively small diameter of approximately 0.5 μm [232]. Individual elastin fibers are predominantly found running parallel to collagen and in the interstices between bands of collagen, and cross-link to form branched networks with adjacent elastin fibers. There may be a higher degree of branching and multidirectionality in the posterior band than in the intermediate zone, where elastin is predominantly oriented in an anteroposterior direction [236]. The peripheral bands contain considerably more elastin than the intermediate zone [220], [235]–[237], and the superior surface contains more than the inferior surface [237].

In the human disc, 69% of the elastin is found in the anterior band, compared with 26% in the posterior band, and 5% in the intermediate zone [237]. Conversely, the porcine disc contains more elastic fibers in the posterior band than other regions [220, 236]. The bilaminar zone and the anterior attachments are significantly more elastin-dense than the disc [234, 237].

Elastin is highly compliant and extensible across a broad elastic region. When considering the dense network of relatively stiff collagen bundles, the sparse network of extensible elastic fibers certainly does not contribute much to the mechanical stiffness or strength of the disc [131]. More likely, elastin aids in restoring the original form after removal of loads [218, 232, 233, 236].

2.3.4   PROTEOGLYCANS AND GLYCOSAMINOGLYCANS

Proteoglycans are ECM molecules that consist of a core protein and at least one branched glycosaminoglycan (GAG) assembly. GAGs are highly negatively charged molecules that, through attractive interactions with water, resist fluid flow, thereby increasing a tissue's compressive integrity. The large proteoglycans bind hundreds of GAG chains and form aggregates by attaching to hyaluronan via link protein (Figure 2.6). These assemblies interweave with the collagen network, becoming effectively immobilized in the ECM due to their size and highly branched structure. Smaller proteoglycans (Figure 2.7), which express collagen binding domains, are believed to regulate fibrillar aggregation, packing density of fibrils [238], and regulate growth factor bioactivity [239].

Much variation exists in the literature for GAG concentration in the disc. Reports have suggested concentrations as high as 10% [240] and as low as 0.5% [216] of total dry weight. Taking into account the whole body of literature, a reasonable approximation would be around 5% of the dry weight [215, 216, 220, 241]. This value represents roughly 10-20% of the GAG concentration typically found in articular cartilage, though it is close to that of the knee meniscus [242]. As with GAG concentration, there is little agreement in the literature regarding the regional distribution of GAG in the disc due to varying test methods and different animal models. Almarza et al. [216]

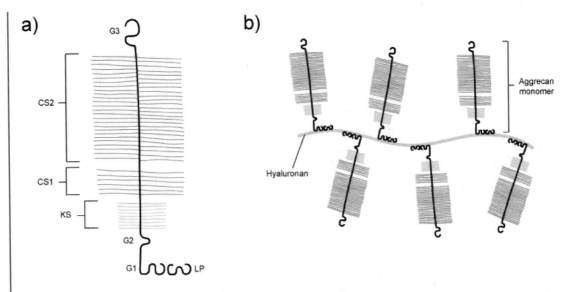

Figure 2.6: Aggrecan, a large aggregating proteoglycan. (a) Aggrecan monomer showing two chondroitin sulfate-rich domains (CS1, CS2), a keratin sulfate rich region (KS), three globular protein domains (G1, G2, G3), and link protein (LP). (b) Several aggrecan monomers binding to hyaluronan to create a large, immobile structure.

found higher GAG content in the medial regions of porcine discs relative to the lateral and central portions, with the posterior band yielding fewer GAGs than central and anterior portions. Detamore et al. [220] had similar findings using porcine discs regarding the distribution of GAGs, though the total content varied between these two studies. Kopp [243] and Nakano and Scott [244] recorded higher GAG content in the central region relative to the periphery in human and bovine discs, respectively. However, Mills et al. [218] found higher concentration of GAGs in the anterior and posterior bands relative to the intermediate zone in the primate TMJ disc. It is possible that the GAG distribution in the disc is heterogeneous and highly variable across these animal models, though a larger study examining an array of animal models using a standardized testing protocol is needed to decisively characterize the distribution of GAGs and proteoglycans in the disc.

The most abundant GAG found in the disc is chondroitin sulfate [215, 220, 240, 241]. The combined total of chondroitin-4 and chondroitin-6-sulfate represents approximately 74-79% of the GAG content in the disc [215, 220, 241]. The majority of these chains are attached to aggrecan [215], the large aggregating proteoglycan found in abundance in hyaline articular cartilage. Keratan sulfate chains, which associate with aggrecan in smaller numbers, constitute approximately 2-9% of the GAG content in the disc [220, 241]. The non-sulfated GAG hyaluronan, which forms the backbone of the aggrecan molecule, is also present in low concentration in the disc constituting between 0.05-10% of the total GAG content [220, 241, 245]. Detamore et al. [220] found a higher

a)

b)

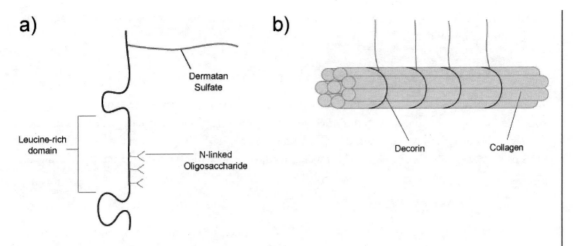

Figure 2.7: The small, leucine-rich proteoglycan, decorin. (a) Decorin molecule showing a leucine-rich domain and a single attached dermatan sulfate molecule. (b) Decorin associating with a collagen bundle.

concentration of chondroitin-6-sulfate in the intermediate and anterior bands than in the posterior band, and found more chondroitin-4-sulfate in the intermediate zone than in the anterior and posterior bands of porcine discs. These results were consistent with an earlier report by Nakano and Scott [244], which showed the concentration of chondroitin sulfate to be 10 times higher in the center relative to the periphery of the bovine disc. Detamore et al. [220] also examined mediolateral variation of chondroitin sulfate concentration, reporting higher values in the medial regions relative to the lateral regions.

In contrast to the chondroitin sulfate proteoglycans (aggrecan, versican), the dermatan sulfate proteoglycans decorin and biglycan are small (~100 kDa) and only bind one or two GAG chains [246]. The biological roles of these proteoglycans remain ill-defined, though regulation of collagen fibrillogenesis is likely a key function. Indeed, the absence of these molecules in knockout mice results in increased variability in collagen fibril size, shape, and aggregation in skin, tendon, and bone, ultimately leading to more brittle tissues [247]. Other purported roles include growth factor modulation and sequestration, and regulation of cell growth [248]. Detamore et al. [220] reported 14.4 and 2.5 times higher dermatan sulfate concentrations in the intermediate zone of porcine discs relative to the posterior and anterior bands, respectively, although no mediolateral differences were found. Scott et al. [249] examined decorin and biglycan individually using gel-electrophoresis and reported roughly equivalent concentrations of biglycan in the central and peripheral regions of bovine discs, but found a higher concentration of decorin in the peripheral tissue relative to the central region. They also noted longer dermatan sulfate chains in the central tissue relative to the outer tissue. Both of these studies reported that dermatan sulfate constitutes about 15% of the total GAG content in the disc [220, 241].

2.4   BIOMECHANICAL PROPERTIES

As discussed in Section 1.6, the TMJ disc experiences tensile, compressive, and shear forces *in situ*. The number of studies devoted to mechanical characterization of the native disc has increased dramatically over the last two decades. This section provides a broad overview of these studies, with particular emphasis on relating biomechanical properties and behavior to the underlying disc structure.

2.4.1   TENSILE PROPERTIES

Upon initial loading, from 0% to ~5% strain, the disc appears to be more compliant than at higher strains. This initial behavior, known as the toe region, has been attributed to the straightening of crimped collagen bundles, and may be correlated with the normal physiological range of motion [230, 231]. After this initial toe region, the disc deforms linearly up to the yield point. Tensile properties are higher when tested parallel to the primary direction of collagen orientation since collagen fibers only resist deformation along their long axis. This is reflected in a number of studies that tested the intermediate zone in the mediolateral direction and found lower stiffness and strength relative to other regions [53, 61, 63, 250]. Teng et al. [250] tested three regions in the canine TMJ disc in the mediolateral direction. The anterior and posterior bands exhibited higher ultimate tensile strength (47 ± 17 and 70 ± 31 MPa) than the intermediate zone (14.7 ± 5.9 MPa), and also yielded a higher elastic modulus (both ~ 30 MPa) than the intermediate zone (18.4 MPa). Beatty et al. [53] tested samples from the central region of the porcine disc in the mediolateral and anteroposterior directions and similarly found the disc to be much softer mediolaterally (7.35 ± 0.23 MPa) than anteroposteriorly (33.8 ± 1.3 MPa).

Detamore et al. [61] tested porcine discs in three directions in both mediolateral and antero-posterior directions under incremental stress relaxation and obtained data for strength, failure energy, and peak and relaxed moduli. In the mediolateral direction, the intermediate zone had the lowest relaxed modulus (0.58 ± 0.39 MPa), followed by the anterior (9.5 ± 3.3 MPa) and posterior (23.4 ± 6.5 MPa) bands. In the anteroposterior direction, the medial and central regions were stiffer than the lateral region, with elastic moduli of 14.3 ± 3.7, 18.5 ± 4.9, and 10.6 ± 3.0 MPa, respectively. The regional peak strengths of the disc ranged from 0.58 MPa to 7.38 MPa, with the weakest being the intermediate zone tested mediolaterally.

Tanaka et al. [45, 64, 251] have performed multiple studies of the TMJ disc in the anteropos-terior direction. In one study [64], bovine discs from three age ranges (young adult, adult, mature adult) were divided into three regions (medial, central, lateral) and loaded at either 1.0 MPa or 1.5 MPa for 20 minutes. Values for the instantaneous modulus were highest in the medial region and lowest in the central region for all three age groups, though the range of values across all groups was relatively small (20.2 - 25.9 MPa). In another study [45], the central and medial regions of human discs from donors ranging from 22-67 years were tested, with values reported for instantaneous modulus varying from 27.1 - 65.2 MPa. Lastly, Tanaka et al. [251] tested healthy human TMJ discs and compared them to those from patients suffering from internal derangement under tensile stress relaxation. They reported a relaxed elastic modulus of 59.2 ± 4.2 MPa for deranged discs compared to 60.5 ± 9.3 MPa for healthy tissue, and instantaneous moduli of 96 ± 17 MPa for deranged and 96 ± 19 MPa for normal discs.

2.4.2   COMPRESSIVE PROPERTIES

Reported values for the compressive modulus of the disc are highly variable, ranging from 16 kPa to 60 MPa [60, 252]. This wide variation can be attributed to interspecies differences, testing method, material model, preconditioning, sample preparation, and environmental conditions. Therefore, the values obtained from these studies should be taken with caution, and more credence should be handed to the regional variation described within an individual work. As a corollary, future characterizations should be performed using uniform testing criteria similar to those set forth by the ASTM for materials testing, or by adapting techniques used for testing other musculoskeletal soft tissues such as tendons or ligaments.

Despite inconsistencies in the literature regarding its compressive properties, it is generally accepted that the disc is likely 10-1000 times softer under compression than tension, with a compressive elastic modulus between 100 kPa and 10 MPa. This difference is stark when comparing to articular cartilage, which displays less of a disparity between moduli under tension and compression [242]. Proteoglycans (aggrecan) are known to increase compressive stiffness by increasing local hydrostatic pressure and impeding fluid flow through the matrix. GAGs play a large role in hyaline articular cartilage mechanics as they compose 15-25% of the tissue's dry weight [253]. As discussed previously, GAGs are relatively sparse in the disc, suggesting its compressive stiffness is dependent on some other structural characteristic. Some important observations were made by Allen et al. [254] after examining the disc's compressive behavior during step-wise stress relaxation tests. First, the relaxation time constants obtained for the disc are substantially shorter than those observed for other cartilaginous tissues (a trait shared by mandibular condylar cartilage as well [255], as noted in Chapter 3). Second, the modulus increases steadily as a function of increasing strain (also observed with mandibular condylar cartilage [255]). The authors attributed short relaxation times to the lack of fluid impedance at low strain levels due to the relative scarcity of GAGs in the tissue. Strain dependence suggests that as the tissue is compressed, collagen fibers become more closely packed together, reducing the effective void space and increasing resistance to fluid flow. Beek et al. [252] hypothesized another mechanism by which collagen might mediate compressive behavior. In their study, whole human discs were dynamically compressed in three regions in the anteroposterior direction, yielding 2 - 3 times higher compressive moduli in the intermediate zone relative to the anterior and posterior bands. To explain these results, the authors proposed a mechanism in which collagen directs fluid flow anteroposteriorly in the intermediate zone during compression up to the bands, where the fluid is obstructed by the mediolaterally oriented collagen fibers. If indeed the compressive properties of the disc are primarily mediated by the underlying collagen structure, then tensile and compressive behaviors are inextricably linked. It is important that future characterizations analyze the interplay of compressive and tensile forces to test these hypotheses and provide a more accurate description of disc behavior *in situ*.

Three studies by Athanasiou's group noted significant compliance in the lateral side of the intermediate zone relative to other regions [60, 254, 256]. First, Kim et al. [60] performed creep indentation tests on the superior surface of the disc and modeled the data using linear biphasic theory. The lateral side of the intermediate zone yielded a significantly lower aggregate modulus (16.3 ± 2.1 kPa) than the medial side (29 ± 12 kPa). Allen and Athanasiou [254, 256] published two studies that tested the surface-regional compressive properties of the disc under step-wise stress relaxation and modeled the data using viscoelastic theory. In both studies, samples from the lateral region demonstrated less mechanical integrity relative to other regions. Along with finite element analyses, which have identified the presence of large forces in the lateral aspects of the disc, these studies provide additional rationalization as to why perforations are preferentially located on the lateral side of the disc [204].

2.4.3   SHEAR AND FRICTIONAL PROPERTIES

The disc is subjected to shearing and frictional forces as a result of translatory and rotational movements during disc loading. The degree of shearing and abrasion in the disc is dependent on multiple factors, including surface roughness and joint lubrication. Lubricating characteristics in the joint are primarily attributed to the presence of synovial fluid, which derives its rheological properties from the unsulfated GAG hyaluronan [257]. In patients suffering from osteoarthrosis, hyaluronan concentration and molecular weight is seen to decrease. Surface roughness can be measured directly using optical profilometry or atomic force microscopy, though no such tests have been performed on the TMJ disc to date. However, several studies have examined the frictional properties of the TMJ disc [258]–[260]. In tests on porcine explants, the frictional coefficient of the disc was determined to be approximately 0.015 - 0.025, increasing with magnitude and time of loading [259]. Another study of porcine discs demonstrated that tractional forces increase with increasing strain and velocity [260].

Large shearing forces are believed to cause deformation and damage in cartilage and fibrocartilage [261] [262, 263], and the TMJ disc is believed to experience some degree of shear loading based on finite element analysis [32, 264]. Nevertheless, only a handful of studies have been published that examined the shear properties of the disc [67, 265, 266]. First, Lai et al. [265] examined regional variation in shear properties of the human TMJ disc using an axiotorsional device. Cylinders were tested from three regions along the mediolateral axis, yielding a shear modulus of around 1.0 MPa for the central region and 1.75 MPa for the medial and lateral regions. Tanaka et al. [67] exposed porcine discs to 0.5% shear strain across a range of loading frequencies (0.1 - 100 Hz) in the mediolateral and anteroposterior directions. The dynamic shear moduli increased non-linearly with increasing frequency. Storage and loss moduli were about 1.5 times greater in the anteroposterior direction relative to the mediolateral direction across the range of frequencies. Tanaka et al. [266] repeated the same procedure in another study but this time varied the compressive strain (5% - 15%) and shear strain (0.5% - 1.5%). Dynamic shear moduli increased with increasing compressive strain, which the authors attributed to a decrease in porosity with increased loading. This result would seem to corroborate the strain dependence of compressive properties [254, 256]. Interestingly, shear moduli decreased with increasing shear strain. The explanation for this behavior is less clear. The authors speculated that water and proteoglycans in the disc may display non-Newtonian shear-softening behavior similar to synovial fluid.

Overall, the frictional and shear properties of the disc remain relatively unknown. It is reasonable to assume that unphysiological shear loading may have a degradative effect, similar to what is seen in other cartilages [262, 263, 267], necessitating the execution of more characterization work. It is likely that disc traction forces increase with the onset of osteoarthrosis as a result of synovial fluid degradation and increased surface roughness. These increased forces could then cause greater shearing in the disc, possibly leading to derangement and disease [50]. An understanding of shear and frictional forces in joint disease processes will no doubt be necessary to avoid premature deterioration of a tissue engineered TMJ disc.

2.5   CELL TYPES

The TMJ disc contains a heterogeneous collection of morphologically variable cells [30]. Some cells are flattened and spindle-shaped much like the tenocytes found in tendons, while others appear rounded, surrounded by a distinct pericellular matrix similar to what is seen in hyaline articular cartilage (Figure 2.8). When taken as a whole population, the TMJ disc cells may be appropriately referred to as *fibrochondrocytes*.

Detamore et al. [268] studied the regional distribution of cells in the porcine disc using histology and transmission electron microscopy, yielding an overall density of 681 ± 197 cells/mm^2, $70\% \pm 11\%$ of which appeared fibroblast-like based on morphology. The intermediate and posterior bands were significantly more cellularized than the anterior band, and the central region of the intermediate zone had approximately 10% fewer cells than the lateral and medial regions. The anterior and posterior bands contained a higher percentage of fibroblasts than the intermediate zone, and the superior and middle layers had higher levels of fibroblast-like cells than the inferior surface. In contrast to these findings, Milam et al. [269] found mostly rounded, chondrocyte-like cells surrounded by lacunae in primate TMJ discs. Mills et al. [218] also reported the presence of rounded, chondrocyte-like cells in the interstices between collagen bundles in primate TMJ discs. Cells were typically found in groups of three to six cells, and were generally smaller and less rounded at the surfaces and close to the peripheral attachments.

Berkovitz and Pacy [270, 271] examined TMJ disc cell anatomy in two studies. The first study [270] explored age-related differences in rats and marmosets, and reported the presence of a microfilamentous pericellular matrix surrounding the cells. This matrix was structurally different from the pericellular matrix of hyaline articular chondrocytes, as it was lacking a pericellular capsule

a)   b)

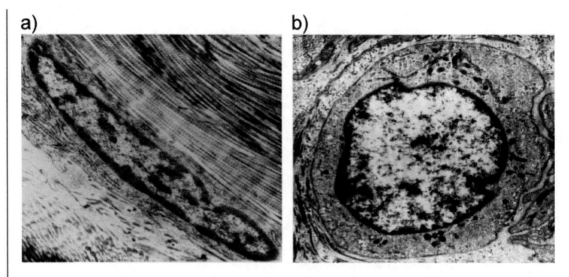

Figure 2.8: Transmission electron micrographs of TMJ disc cells. (a) A spindle-shaped cell and (b) a rounded cell.

separating the cells from the ECM. Perhaps the most interesting finding was a transition in cell morphology from a fibrous cell to a more chondrocyte-like morphology with advancing age. In the second study [271], the authors examined mature adult human discs removed due to TMJ dysfunction, though the investigation only focused on areas of tissue that appeared to be the least affected by disease processes. The cells in this study were oval-shaped, contained only moderate amounts of intracellular organelles, and were characterized by a large volume of filamentous material that filled the cytoplasm. Cells lacked a distinct pericellular matrix similar to those seen in the previous study [270], and most cells were found closely associated with the collagen fiber network. Cell appearance in this study would suggest the human disc at advanced age is more fibrous than fibrocartilaginous. However, the authors correctly note that it would be inappropriate to assume equivalence between apparently non-affected regions of a diseased disc and a wholly undamaged tissue.

In vitro examinations of the metabolic processes of isolated TMJ disc cells give clues to their phenotype and *in situ* functional roles [218, 219, 272, 273]. Mills et al. [272] cultured rabbit cells from both the disc and its fibrous attachments. Cells isolated from the disc maintained a polygonal morphology and synthesized cartilage-like proteoglycans, while cells derived from the attachments were spindle shaped and produced fibroblast-like proteoglycans. A later study by Mills et al. [218] confirmed these reports, as cells from primate discs maintained a polygonal shape during *in vitro* culture. Landesberg et al. [219] analyzed cell proliferation, collagen synthesis, proteoglycan synthesis, and RNA in cultured bovine disc cells. Disc cells proliferated very rapidly in culture, much faster than chondrocytes. Cells synthesized collagen as 12% of total protein produced, similar to what is seen for cultured articular chondrocytes. Collagen type II RNA was found, though at low levels relative to control mandibular condyle cells. Kapila et al. [273] cultured leporine disc cells and assessed the conditioned media for proteinases using polyacrylamide gels followed by western blots. They noted the presence of several matrix metalloproteinases (MMPs), including gelatinase, procollagenase and prostromelysin. They also isolated two proteinases inhibitors, most likely TIMP and TIMP-2, using reverse zymography. These findings suggest disc cells contribute to ECM remodeling though secretion of MMPs, and additionally, they express an MMP profile more reflective of a synovial fibroblast than a chondrocyte.

In summary, there is no single description of the phenotype of a TMJ disc cell. Instead, the cells should be viewed as a heterogeneous distribution expressing characteristics that fit somewhere along the phenotypic spectrum between a fibroblast and a chondrocyte. Therefore, the term *fibrochondrocyte* most accurately describes the heterogeneous population of TMJ disc cells [219].

2.6   AGE-ASSOCIATED CHANGES IN THE DISC

The mechanical strength and stiffness of many connective tissues, such as articular cartilage, skin, and bone, increase into adulthood, then gradually decrease with advancing age [43, 274, 275]. However, several studies indicate that the mechanical integrity of the TMJ disc is sustained or continues to increase past the point of skeletal maturation [45, 64, 126, 265, 276]. Tanaka et al. [64, 126, 276] examined the tensile, compressive, and dynamic viscoelastic properties of discs from young-adult (3 year-old), adult (7 year-old), and mature-adult (10 year-old) cattle. Under creep tension [276], mature-adult discs were around 10% stiffer than adult discs and also maintained the least residual strain after unloading. For compressive stress relaxation [126], the instantaneous (17 MPa) and relaxed moduli (4 MPa) were similar between adult and mature-adult groups. Under dynamic (cyclical) compressive loads applied at 1 Hz [64], the storage modulus of young-adult discs (0.69 MPa) was significantly smaller than that of adult (1.21 MPa) and mature-adult (1.44 MPa) discs. In addition, the loss modulus for the mature-adult group (0.23 MPa) was significantly larger than the loss moduli of the younger groups. In a study of discs from human donors, Tanaka et al. [45] reported a significant correlation ($p < 0.01$) between aging (range 22 - 67) and tensile modulus (27.1 - 65.2 MPa). Finally, Lai et al. [265] found the shear modulus of human discs increased significantly ($p < 0.01$) with increasing age (range 36 - 76).

Age-related changes in mechanical properties are accompanied by, and can be largely attributed to, changes in ECM composition and organization. Nakano and Scott [244] quantified the biochemical composition of bovine discs, separated into inner and peripheral regions, from prenatal development through maturation. In both regions, collagen content increased rapidly during prenatal development, then plateaued thereafter, while water concentration decreased steadily, though not significantly, from fetus to adult. Most notably, there was a dramatic increase in chondroitin sulfate (13-fold) and keratan sulfate (1600-fold) concentration from immature to mature adult in the inner tissue, though the outer tissue remained relatively constant in this regard. The authors hypothesized that increased GAG concentration was an adaptive response to cyclic compressive loading, which occurs predominantly in the central region of this disc. Indeed, it has been shown that direct compression of disc explants leads to increased production of chondroitin sulfate [277], that cyclic compression increases production of GAGs in articular cartilage *in vitro* [278, 279], and that moderate exercise stimulates GAG production *in vivo* [280]. A higher concentration of GAGs would reduce the mechanical load-carriage requirement of the solid matrix by increasing interstitial fluid pressure, thus allowing more energy dissipation through viscous effects.

Collagen microarchitecture also undergoes significant changes during maturation and aging. Ahn et al. [281] examined collagen fibril size and arrangement in the intermediate zone of rat discs aged 1 day to 1 year using quantitative analysis of scanning electron micrographs. From birth up to 2 weeks, individual fibrils were 45 ± 3 nm in diameter. At 4 weeks, smaller and larger fibrils had deposited, which doubled the standard deviation, though the average size remained the same. By 8 weeks, the average fibril diameter increased to 58 ± 19 nm, with a similar value shown for the 1 year samples. A broad distribution of sizes could clearly be seen in the electron micrographs at 1 year, and the packing density was much higher than in younger tissue, where uniformly-sized fibrils were separated by regular void spaces. A broadening distribution of fibril diameters in collagen bundles during development is typical of all collagenous tissues, and tensile load-bearing tissues such as tendon also show an increasing fibril diameter during postnatal development [282, 283]. Larger fibril diameter is correlated with increased tissue stiffness and a reduction in extensibility, as evidenced by a shortened toe region [283]. In the same way that increased deposition of GAGs is a response to cyclic compressive loading, an increase in disc fibril diameter is likely a response to cyclic tensile stresses during mastication.

Greater levels of calcium in the disc are correlated with advancing age [43]. Jibiki et al. [44] showed calcifications in 37% of discs obtained from cadaveric donors of ages 47 to 107 using x-ray radiography and electron microscopy. In this study, calcium deposits were associated with legions predominantly located in the posterior band. The majority of these deposits had structures characteristic of an endochondral ossification process, including lamellae, thick collagen fibers, Haversian canals, and lacunae. Previous studies found similar features in discs from patients with TMD [284, 285]. Though calcifications were related to arthropathy or mechanical injury in this study, it is possible that calcification is inherent to the aging process.

In summary, the composition and structure of disc ECM changes in response to mechanical stresses during the aging process, and these changes are manifested in increased mechanical stiffness and strength. Collagen concentration increases and fibrils widen and become more densely packed, leading to increased tensile modulus and strength. Increased calcification may also contribute to increased mechanical properties. GAG concentration in the compressively loaded intermediate zone rises with age, leading to higher compressive and viscous properties. Considerable evidence suggests this adaptation process continues past the point of skeletal maturity.

CHAPTER 3

Cartilage of the Mandibular Condyle

3.1   INTRODUCTION

The previous chapter reviewed the composition and mechanical properties of the TMJ disc. In comparison, there are far fewer characterization studies available for the mandibular condylar cartilage, with regard to both composition and biomechanics. However, there are a number of both interesting similarities and distinct differences between these two tissues. It is not surprising that the mandibular condylar cartilage shares many structural similarities with the TMJ disc, given their close anatomical relationship and coupled function in the TMJ. For example, both the TMJ disc and mandibular condyle are wider mediolaterally than anteroposteriorly. Moreover, the circumferential and anteroposterior organization of predominantly type I collagen fibers observed in the TMJ disc is also observed in the superficial zone of the condylar cartilage. One distinction between the two tissues is that the condylar cartilage is considerably thinner than the TMJ disc, as reports of condylar cartilage thickness have ranged from 200 - 780 μm [255], [286]–[290]. Another important distinction is the obvious difference of the subchondral bone underlying the condylar cartilage. This structure imparts on the condylar cartilage a zonal organization that is reminiscent of, yet clearly distinct from, hyaline cartilage. Although there have been a number of classification schemes that describe this zonal organization [201], [292]–[299], the following sections will utilize the four-zone nomenclature of the fibrous, proliferative, mature and hypertrophic zones (Figure 3.1). Generally, speaking, the fibrous zone is a fibrocartilaginous region similar in many ways to the TMJ disc, separated by the thin and highly cellular proliferative zone from the underlying hyaline-like mature and hypertrophic zones. In terms of regions, as opposed to the zones, the condylar cartilage is often arbitrarily divided into the posterior, superior (central), and anterior regions, with no particular anatomical distinction between regions.

Extensive reviews summarizing the biochemical content and biomechanical properties of the condylar cartilage are available in the literature [297, 298]. The remainder of this chapter is intended to familiarize the reader with a comprehensive overview of salient structural and functional characteristics of the condylar cartilage.

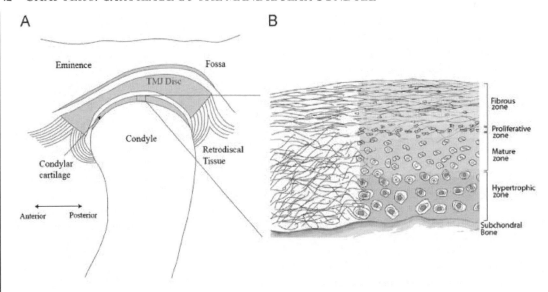

Figure 3.1: Schematic of condylar cartilage. (A) Location of condylar cartilage in the human TMJ relative to the condyle, disc, and eminence-fossa. (B) Schematic of the zonal organization of condylar cartilage, showing fibrous, proliferative, mature, and hypertrophic zones. (Obtained with permission from Singh and Detamore, J Biomech, 2009 [297].)

3.2   BIOCHEMICAL CONTENT

3.2.1   COLLAGEN COMPOSITION AND DISTRIBUTION

Collagen type I is found throughout all zones of the mandibular condylar cartilage, although collagen type II predominates in the mature and hypertrophic zones. More specifically, collagen type I has been detected immunohistochemically in the condylar cartilage of rats [293, 300, 301], baboons [269], and pigs [302], as the predominant collagen type in the fibrous zone but found only in localized regions (e.g., pericellular matrix) in the mature and hypertrophic zones. In contrast, immunohistochemical data have shown that the collagen of the mature and hypertrophic zones is predominately type II, whereas the fibrous zone is virtually free of collagen type II [293], [301]–[303]. In addition to these primary collagen types, immunohistochemical evaluations of rat condylar cartilage have found collagen type X in the mature and hypertrophic zones [303], and collagen type III in the fibrous zone [301]. It appears that although collagen is by far the most abundant ECM constituent, very little is known about the actual percent dry weight of collagen in the condylar cartilage, much less the regional variations of collagen content. However, a figure of 165.7 nmol hydroxyproline/mg dry-weight guanidium chloride extract has been reported [304], and a value of 2.2 μg/mg wet weight (via hydroxyproline assay) was provided more recently. Furthermore, in discussing collagen distribution in the mandibular condylar cartilage, one cannot overlook the pioneering efforts of de Bont and colleagues [305], who also made important early contributions to collagen fiber organization in the TMJ disc [228]. They observed that in contrast to the fibrous, mature and hypertrophic zones, the proliferative zone is primarily a cellular region with relatively few collagen fibers [305].

3.2.2 COLLAGEN ORGANIZATION

Collagen fibrils in mandibular condylar cartilage have been reported to vary from 30 - 180 nm in diameter, with collagen fibers ranging from 1 - 4 μm [300, 306, 307]. These numbers are similar to the fiber diameters reviewed for the TMJ disc in the previous chapter. Berkovitz [230, 231], who also investigated collagen crimping in the TMJ disc, reported a mean crimp periodicity of 19.4 μm for collagen of the condylar cartilage [231], comparable to the 8 - 23 μm range for the TMJ disc presented in the previous chapter.

For many years, studies of collagen fiber orientation in the condylar cartilage were microscopic investigations. These studies collectively found that collagen fibers of the fibrous zone appeared to run predominately parallel to the surface but not to each other, forming sheet-like structures [292, 300], [305]–[307], which would suggest a transversely isotropic orientation. However, it was not until 2008 that a macroscopic investigation via polarized light microscopy revealed a highly anisotropic organization of collagen fibers in the fibrous zone that was remarkably similar to that of the TMJ disc [61, 62].

In contrast to the fibrous zone, collagen fiber orientation is more isotropic in the three underlying zones. The mature and hypertrophic zones appeared to exhibit an arrangement of randomly oriented bundles [300, 305], and the few collagen fibers observed in the proliferative zone were mostly scattered individual fibers with occasional fiber bundles [300, 306].

Finally, in addition to collagen fibers, elastic fibers were observed in all zones of rat condylar cartilage, with longitudinal, oblique and transverse orientations, and fibril and fiber diameters of 8 nm and 350 nm, respectively, [308].

3.2.3 PROTEOGLYCANS AND GLYCOSAMINOGLYCANS

Quantitative data on the glycosaminoglycan content of mandibular condylar cartilage are scarce. Two studies have measured similar absolute masses of sulfated glycosaminoglycans in rabbits, with values of 0.19 mg [304] and 0.18 mg [309]. In terms of a wet weight concentration, a value of 6.6 μg/mg was reported in rats [301].

As with all other facets of the condylar cartilage, proteoglycan content varies depending on the zone. For example, immunohistochemical investigations of porcine [310] and rat [303] condylar cartilages found that aggrecan was localized primarily in the mature and hypertrophic zones. In addition, chondroitin sulfate rich versican-like proteoglycans were observed in the fibrous and proliferative zones in porcine [310] and rat [311] models. However, there is contradictory evidence in the literature pertaining to the distribution of keratan and chondroitin sulfate. A primate study found these glycosaminoglycans confined to the mature and hypertrophic zones [269], unlike in porcine and rat studies [310, 311]. In addition to zonal differences, there appear to be regional differences in proteoglycan distribution as well. It appears that in rabbit condylar cartilage, the posterosuperior and anterior regions contain more chondroitin sulfate rich proteoglycans than the superior region [312, 313].

Little is known about the dermatan sulfate proteoglycan content of the condylar cartilage, other than a report that decorin content increases with age in a rat model [314]. It is clear that a more comprehensive regional and zonal characterization is required to gain a true appreciation for the zonal and regional distribution of proteoglycans in the condylar cartilage. One might speculate, given the fibrocartilaginous nature of the fibrous zone and the hyaline-like nature of the underlying mature and hypertrophic zones, that the fibrous zone would contain more decorin, just as the mature and hypertrophic zones appear to contain more aggrecan.

3.3 BIOMECHANICAL PROPERTIES

It would appear that compression may be the primary form of loading on the condylar bone, based on *in vivo* strain measurements on the condylar neck during mastication in pigs [76, 77], and also on the structure of the bone [315, 316]. The condylar cartilage of course would be involved in transmitting that compressive stress to the underlying bone, although the cartilage experiences direct shear and thus tensile forces with its articulation against the TMJ disc. Although studies of the biomechanical properties of condylar cartilage are scarce, there are studies that cover its tensile, shear, and compressive properties. For a more in depth review of condylar cartilage biomechanics studies through early 2009, an extensive review is available in the literature [317].

3.3.1 TENSILE AND SHEAR PROPERTIES

There are two tensile studies and shear studies of the condylar cartilage, all of which were performed with a porcine model. Kang et al. [318] tested eight condylar cartilage-bone specimens under uniaxial tension to failure, four in the mediolateral direction and four in the anteroposterior direction. Regional variation was not tested in either direction. The key finding in this study was that condylar cartilage was stiffer and stronger in the anteroposterior direction than in the mediolateral direction (Young's moduli of 9.0 and 6.5 MPa, respectively). This anisotropic tensile behavior would suggest a macroscopic anisotropic collagen fiber orientation, although this orientation was not confirmed until several years later [62]. The anisotropy under tension was also confirmed in another study, with mediolateral moduli ranging from 8 to 11 MPa (Young's) and 3.6 to 3.9 MPa (equilibrium), and anteroposterior moduli ranging from 22 to 29 MPa (Young's) and 6.2 to 8.8 MPa (equilibrium) [62]. Unlike the TMJ disc, as reviewed in the previous chapter, the condylar cartilage appears to exhibit less regional variation within each direction.

Tanaka and colleagues [70, 319] have performed shear tests that have further confirmed the anisotropy observed under tension. These dynamic shear experiments at a frequency of 2 Hz revealed storage moduli ranging from 1.50 to 2.03 MPa in the anteroposterior direction and 0.33 to 0.55 MPa in the mediolateral direction. Clearly, the TMJ disc and the condylar cartilage are stiffer under tension and shear in the anteroposterior direction than in the mediolateral direction, which we propose is the result of a predominately anteroposterior movement of the condyle.

3.3.2 COMPRESSIVE PROPERTIES

Compressive studies of the condylar cartilage have included indentation of porcine tissue [69, 291, 320], atomic force microscopy on rabbit tissue [321, 322], and unconfined compression on porcine tissue [255]. In one study, four regions of rabbit condylar cartilage were investigated, and a heterogeneity was revealed that suggested the cartilage was stiffer medially than laterally [322]. An early regional macroscopic indentation study demonstrated that dynamic moduli (complex, storage, and loss) were higher in the anterior region than in the posterior region [69], in agreement with nanoindentation findings [322].

Regional relaxed moduli with porcine condylar cartilage have been reported in terms of aggregate moduli from an *in situ* creep test [291] and in terms of equilibrium moduli from explanted unconfined compression tests [255]. Variations between these two studies included the strain (50% for stress relaxation, approximately 13 to 22% strain calculated from available data for creep) and measured cartilage thickness (0.4 to 0.8 mm for stress relaxation, 1.0 to 2.3 mm for creep). The aggregate moduli ranged from 45 to 75 kPa, with the central and medial regions being highest. The equilibrium moduli ranged from 9 to 23 kPa (and corresponding elastic moduli ranged from 0.8 to 1.5 Mpa), with the posterior region being stiffest and the anterior region being most compliant. One clear point of agreement between these two studies was that the anterior region was the thinnest.

In summary, the condylar cartilage is a thin, heterogeneous tissue. Like the TMJ disc, more data are required to come to a consensus with regard to the exact regional variations in the compressive behavior of the condylar cartilage. Studies on healthy human tissues would be particularly valuable, given that all compressive data to date are derived from animals.

3.4 CELL CONTENT

The cells of the fibrous zone appear to be primarily fibroblast-like cells [307, 308]. The underlying proliferative zone is a highly cellular region, which aids in producing cells for the fibrous zone [307, 323, 324]. The proliferative zone is essentially a cell reservoir for the condylar cartilage, with mesenchymal chondrocyte precursors for the underlying zones as well [288, 325, 326]. With the cells being responsible for the adaptation of the matrix content and organization in response to the loading environment, the proliferative zone, despite its relatively small volume, must certainly play an important role in adaptation [326]. In the mature and hypertrophic zones, the cells are predominantly mature chondrocytes [306].

The zonal organization of cell types is consistent with the zonal variation in matrix composition as described earlier in this chapter. The chondrocytes, aggrecan, and collagen II content of the mature and hypertrophic zones are reminiscent of hyaline cartilages, whereas the fibroblast-like cells, and highly aligned collagen type I fibers of the fibrous zone are more similar to fibrous tissues and the TMJ disc.

CHAPTER 4

Tissue Engineering of the Disc

4.1 INTRODUCTION

An *in vitro* tissue engineering approach is shown in Figure 4.1. Cells are seeded on an appropriate scaffold and then cultured in an environment that promotes production of native ECM tissue, leading to tissue-specific biomechanical characteristics. The initial choice of a particular cell, scaffold, or exogenous stimulation regimen is based on characterization data, native tissue development, or engineering studies of other tissues. As attempts are made and studies are published, techniques become more refined to a point where a construct ready for *in vivo* implantation and testing is produced. Whereas these aspects have become increasingly well defined for articular cartilage and bone tissue engineering, significant questions regarding cell source, scaffold choice, and stimulation regimen still remain for the TMJ disc.

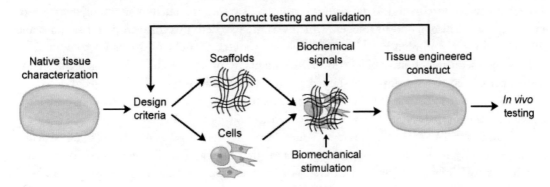

Figure 4.1: A roadmap for tissue engineering the TMJ disc.

From 1991-2001, four articles were published that suggested it would be possible to engineer a cartilaginous tissue in the shape of a TMJ disc [8]–[10], [123]. Since that time, numerous studies have considered scaffolding options, biomechanical stimulation regimens, growth factor strategies, and alternative cell sources toward the goal of recapitulating the biochemical and biomechanical properties of the native disc in tissue engineered constructs. These studies will be introduced in the following section to provide researchers a base from which to devise a well-informed *in vitro* tissue engineering strategy. Following that section, there will be sections on scaffold selection, biochemical factors, and bioreactors that draw on insights garnered from tissue engineering studies of the TMJ disc and other cartilaginous tissues.

4.2   PREVIOUS TISSUE ENGINEERING EFFORTS

Thomas et al. [8] published the first *in vitro* TMJ disc tissue engineering study in 1991. In this study, second passage leporine disc cells were suspended with unpolymerized collagen type I and allowed to polymerize after injection in a porous collagen matrix. The constructs underwent a significant change in size over two weeks, decreasing from 16 to 12 mm in diameter. Cells cultured in collagen scaffolds were more chondrocytic than monolayer controls, exhibiting a rounded morphology and staining positively for proteoglycans. Three years later, Puelacher et al. [9] created human disc-shaped constructs by seeding primary bovine articular chondrocytes on pre-shaped polylactic acid/polyglycolic acid (PLA/PGA) scaffolds. After 1 week of *in vitro* culture, constructs were implanted subcutaneously in nude mice and cultured *in vivo* for 12 weeks. Histological staining of constructs revealed the presence of GAGs and collagen II, and most significantly, the constructs retained their shape after the culture period.

Girdler [10] created disc-shaped constructs from mandibular cartilage cells of marmosets. The author indicated that chondroprogenitor cells were isolated but did not specify the zone from which these cells were procured, or provided verification that they were, in fact, chondrocyte progenitors. The isolated cells were expanded in monolayer for 3 weeks, maintaining a polygonal morphology throughout the culture period. After trypsinization, cells were suspended in an unpolymerized solution of type I collagen and fibrinogen, which was then seeded into collagen type I sponges and polymerized using thrombin in sodium chloride and sodium citrate. Constructs were cultured for 14 days, then semi-quantitative biochemical assessments for proteoglycans and collagen types I and II were performed. These constructs stained positively for collagen type II and proteoglycans, and round-shaped cells were embedded within a dense matrix. Despite the thorough histological matrix assessment, the mechanical integrity of these constructs was not assessed.

Springer et al. [123] sought to create a durable replacement disc by culturing disc and articular eminence cells from humans and pigs on non-absorbent scaffolds, including expanded polytetrafluoroethylene (ePTFE) monofilaments, PGA monofilaments, polyamide monofilaments, and bone mineral blocks. The idea was that these scaffolds would provide a stress-absorbing framework within a tissue engineered construct. Isolated cells were expanded for one passage, and then seeded in scaffolds for 2 hours before medium containing 10% serum was added. Constructs were cultured for 2, 4, or 8 weeks in the same medium, then evaluated using electron microscopy and gel electrophoresis. Cells from human and pig sources showed no differences in monolayer culture or on scaffolding material. Cells became confluent on scaffolds within 4 weeks, assuming either a spherical or fusiform shape. SDS-PAGE revealed the presence of collagen type II, suggesting the cells were of a chondrocytic phenotype. Polyamide and ePTFE scaffolds did not degrade over the culture period, though PGA fibers showed fissures within 4 weeks and were mechanically unstable at 8 weeks. One large concern for the future applicability of this study is the biocompatibility of the polyamide and ePTFE scaffolds. Though these materials did not degrade in this study, some degradation could occur after continued exposure to the mechanical forces present in the joint, leading to formation of wear particles and subsequent foreign-body responses, as discussed in Chapter 1.

From 2004-2008, Athanasiou et al. [2]–[4], [15]–[19], [327]–[331] published 13 articles refining the use of porcine TMJ disc cells for tissue engineering. These studies optimized monolayer culture conditions, scaffold selection, seeding density and technique, growth factor regimens, and biomechanical stimulation regimens. The first scaffold used was alginate, though it was unsuccessful due to a marked decrease in cell number and a lack of ECM production [2]. PGA nonwoven meshes were seeded successfully using spinner-flasks, and constructs produced significantly higher levels of collagen type I relative to PGA scaffolds seeded using other methods [2]. Cell seeding density was then optimized, noting that initial seeding should not exceed 75 million cells/mL of scaffold volume [3]. Later, a poly-L-lactic-acid (PLLA) scaffold was tested in an effort to limit construct contraction, hypothesizing that its slower degradation rate would allow for significant matrix deposition and thereby increase the mechanical integrity of constructs [331]. At 4 weeks, PGA constructs had contracted to roughly 5% of their original volume, while PLLA constructs retained their initial dimensions.

Several growth factors were tested for their effects on disc cells in monolayer and in scaffolds. First, the growth factors IGF-I, PDGF, and bFGF were examined at concentrations of 10 and 100 ng/mL for their effects on cell proliferation and matrix production after 14 days of monolayer culture [15]. All growth factors increased the proliferation rate relative to controls. PDGF and bFGF induced a more than two-fold increase in GAG production relative to controls, and IGF-I and bFGF increased production of collagen. In general, higher growth factor concentrations enhanced cell proliferation while the lower concentrations increased biosynthesis. Next, IGF-I, bFGF, and TGF-β1 were added at two concentrations during 3-D culture [327]. All growth factor groups had improved mechanical and structural integrity relative to controls, and IGF-I and TGF-β1 were shown to increase collagen synthesis. Combinations of these three growth factors were then assessed [4]. All combinations improved cellularity and mechanical integrity, though no single combination stood out as particularly beneficial. Finally, IGF-I, TGF-β1, and TGF-β3 were tested on PLLA-seeded constructs [331]. Constructs treated with TGF-β1 had double the number of cells and GAG content and 15 times the collagen content of those treated with IGF-I. This finding was particularly interesting, considering these two growth factors behaved similarly when tested on PGA-seeded constructs [327]. This dramatic difference could be a result of changes in the local pH due to degradation rates, or as a result of the dynamic cell density changes due to PGA contraction.

Almarza and Athanasiou [18] examined the effects of cyclic and constant hydrostatic pressure on disc cells. A 10 MPa amplitude treatment was applied for 4 hours at 0 and 1 Hz to cells in monolayer to test for gene expression of cartilaginous matrix components. Cyclic application resulted in increased collagen type II and decreased collagen type I, aggrecan, and decorin expression relative to controls, while constant application increased collagen type I and decreased aggrecan expression. Next, these treatments were applied intermittently over 1 week to measure matrix production in 3-D constructs. Constant application increased collagen production (24.5 μg/construct) relative to controls (18.2 μg/construct) and groups receiving cyclic treatment (7.5 μg/construct). Detamore and Athanasiou [19] tested the effectiveness of a rotating wall bioreactor, which had been shown to enhance biosynthesis and improve matrix homogeneity in articular chondrocyte-seeded constructs. The results of this study did not support its future use with these cells, however, as statically cultured constructs generally outperformed the rotating groups.

The stability of the TMJ disc cell phenotype during *in vitro* culture was examined in three studies [17, 328, 330]. Gene expression did not vary depending on the region of the disc from which cells were isolated, though cells were found to rapidly down-regulate aggrecan, collagen type I, and collagen type II expression with passage [17]. Expansion of cells would be necessary to obtain enough cells for creation of a full-sized autologous construct; therefore attempts were made to recover the lost phenotype. Cells passaged up to five times were exposed to the growth factors IGF-I, TGF-β1, and TGF-β3 for 24 hours in monolayer or pellet culture and analyzed using real time RT-PCR [328]. The growth factors did not have a positive effect on cells cultured using either method, and pellet culture had a negative effect on expression relative to monolayer. Recovery of phenotype was then attempted through culture on ECM coated surfaces [330]. Passage 0, 1, and 2 cells were plated on surfaces coated with aggrecan, collagen type I, collagen type II, or decorin, though no treatment had a significantly positive effect.

More recently, a series of studies were published that suggested that costal cartilage could serve as an autologous cell source for disc tissue engineering [1], [332]–[334]. This tissue would be particularly appealing as many craniofacial surgeons have experience replacing the mandible with a rib graft. In one study [333], scaffoldless constructs (see *scaffolds* section below) were created from primary and passaged goat costal chondrocytes (CCs), and compared to control TMJ disc cells. Cellularity and GAG content of primary and passaged CCs constructs were nearly an order of magnitude higher than disc-cell constructs after 6 weeks of culture, and most importantly, CC constructs retained their size and shape throughout the culture period (∼3 mm dia.), while disc-cell constructs contracted severely (0.84 mm dia.). Immunostaining revealed the presence of collagen types I and II throughout primary CC constructs, though constructs from passaged cells only stained around the periphery and in the middle where a large, fluid-filled core had formed. This sphere did not form in primary CC or disc-cell constructs. Not surprisingly, similar results were observed when mandibular condylar cartilage cells were compared directly to hyaline cartilage cells from the ankle [302, 335], with hyaline cartilage cells outperforming the TMJ cells (see Chapter 5).

4.3   SCAFFOLDS

The purpose of a scaffold is to provide a vehicle upon which cells may grow and deposit matrix. A suitable scaffold must be biocompatible, sterilizable, and biodegradable. It must be sufficiently porous and allow unrestricted cell growth and diffusion of nutrients through large, interconnected pores [336]. The physical properties of the scaffold should support matrix deposition, and the degradation profile should allow newly deposited matrix to gradually assume mechanical loads. Additionally, there should be a method for which the size and shape of the scaffold can be modified to fit the specific dimensions of the target tissue. It may also be advantageous for a scaffold to direct cellular processes though the release of growth factors, or by providing mechanical feedback through cell-substrate interactions.

Synthetic scaffolds are highly versatile. The shape and size can be modified to fit specific applications. Important characteristics, such as porosity, mechanical properties, degradation rate, and hydrophilicity, can be tuned by modifying production procedures or by creation of custom copolymers. PLA and PGA are two widely used biodegradable and biocompatible scaffolding materials. In addition to their use in previous TMJ disc tissue engineering studies, they have also been tested for regeneration of the knee meniscus [337]–[339] and intervertebral disc [112, 340, 341]. These polymers are hydrolyzed into lactic acid and glycolic acid, which are then metabolized further by the body and excreted [342]. A primary difference between these two scaffolds is the degradation rate. Initial PLA degradation products are larger and do not diffuse as readily as PGA products, and therefore PLA degrades more slowly [331]. The previous work with PGA demonstrated that its degradation rate was far too fast at its given formulation and structure for use with TMJ disc cells, however PLA/PGA copolymers or higher molecular weight polymers could show promise for future work. Polyurethane materials such as polycaprolactone (PCL) have been explored for engineered menisc [343, 344] and mandibular condyles [27] due to their slow degradation rate and high mechanical properties. Foams made from these materials and copolymers of PCL and PLA can be formed to any size or shape; porosity and degradation rate can be adjusted by modifying molecular weight/intrinsic viscosity, composition, and fabrication method. Because of the existence of literature based on the use of polyurethane polymers for meniscus and mandibular condyle tissue engineering, studies examining their possible use for TMJ disc tissue engineering are warranted.

The most extensively studied scaffolding material for cartilage tissue engineering is collagen [345]. Type I collagen is most commonly used due to its abundance. The collagen can be used either intact or after proteolytic digestion, allowing for formation of gels. Gels have shown promise for repair of cartilage defects functioning as delivery systems for injectable cell suspensions [346], though this approach would not work for the TMJ disc. A more realistic approach for the disc would involve the use of prefabricated collagen sponges [347]. These scaffolds are highly porous (>95%) and have pore diameters greater than 120 μm. A possible limitation for collagen and other natural scaffolds, such as hyaluronan and alginate, is their inherently low rigidity [348]. Constructs may not retain their shape in light of past experiences with PGA.

Another possible approach involves the use of decellularized tissues, such as periosteal tissue [349], perichondrial tissue [350], and small intestine submucosa [351] to serve as scaffolds. Of course, the porosity and shape of these tissues cannot be varied to recreate the specific morphology of the disc. Lumpkins et al. [352] proposed using a decellularized porcine disc as a xenogenic scaffold, comparable to approaches seen with other tissues such as heart valves [353]. In this study, discs decellularized with sodium dodecyl sulfate (SDS) maintained their size and shape, and displayed similar mechanical energy dissipation characteristics similar to the native disc. This study was published very recently, and the future utility of these scaffolds is unknown, as these constructs have yet to be tested with cells.

Though the byproducts of polymer degradation are non-toxic, they are acidic in the case of aliphatic polyesters, such as PGA and PLA and their copolymers, and cause a drop in pH in the local environment. This acidity could potentially have deleterious effects on cells. In addition, scaffolds may shield cells from stresses imparted from bioreactors or from the *in vivo* environment, thereby preventing mechanotransductive events. Therefore, efforts have been made to devise a method for scaffoldless tissue engineering [5]. One such process, termed the self-assembly process, involves seeding cells at a high density in non-adherent agarose wells, and has been used to create tissue engineered articular cartilage constructs with clinically relevant dimensions (15 mm dia. and 1 mm thick), and aggregate modulus approaching 1/3 that of native tissue [5]. This technique has also been used to fabricate semilunar knee menisci using co-cultures of articular chondrocytes and meniscal fibrochondrocytes [354]. By using an appropriate mold shape, along with cells that can survive in a scaffold-free environment, self assembly could prove to be a successful approach for engineering the TMJ disc.

4.4 BIOACTIVE AGENTS

The effects of growth factors on TMJ disc cells and disc-cell seeded constructs have been studied previously. The specific growth factors examined include TGF-β1, TGF-β3, PDGF, bFGF, and IGF-1. Salient results are presented in Table 4.1. Perhaps the most important finding from these studies is that higher concentrations of growth factors tend to increase cell proliferation, while lower concentrations enhance biosynthesis [355]. Therefore, a good approach might be to expose constructs to high levels of growth factors upon seeding to increase cellularity, and then gradually reduce the concentration to encourage ECM deposition.

Biochemical agents other than growth factors may have utility for TMJ disc tissue engineering. Natoli et al. [356] found that the GAG-depleting agent chondroitinase-ABC can be used to increase tensile properties in scaffoldless tissue engineered cartilage constructs. This process involves temporarily removing GAGs to allow for enhanced organization and alignment of the collagen network. Also, the pro-inflammatory cytokine interleukin-1 (IL-1) has been shown to encourage migration of meniscal fibrochondrocytes [357]. Future tissue engineering studies should examine the use of catabolic treatments for matrix modification and cell signaling, in addition to the more widely studied anabolic factors.

4.5 MECHANICAL STIMULATION AND BIOREACTORS

Because of their inherent avascularity, cartilaginous tissues require mechanical loading to exchange nutrients and waste products. In addition, biomechanical stimuli may be essential for cell survival and matrix synthesis, as unused cartilage atrophies [358]. The TMJ disc is exposed to direct forces imparted through contact with the condyle and fossa, and hydrostatic loading from fluid pressurization in the joint capsule. As discussed in Chapter 2, a lifetime of exposure to forces leads to changes

Table 4.1: Effects of growth factors on TMJ disc cells

Growth factor	Concentrations	Cell source	Notable effects	Ref.
In monolayer				
TGF-β1	0.03 - 3 ng/mL	Cow	250% increase in cell number	[219]
bFGF	3 ng/mL	Cow	Upregulation of Erk1/2 and p38	[355]
	10, 100 ng/mL	Pig	96% increase in cell number	[15]
			280% increase in GAG	
			420% increase in collagen	
IGF-1	10, 100 ng/mL	Pig	49% increase in cell number	[15]
			270% increase in GAG	
			450% increase in collagen	
PDGF	20 ng/mL	Cow	Upregulation of Erk1/2 and p38	[355]
	10, 100 ng/mL	Pig	41% increase in cell number	[15]
In 3-D culture				
TGF- β1	5, 30 ng/mL	Pig	110% increase in collagen	[327]
	5 ng/mL	Pig	Maintained cellularity	[331]
			10-fold increase in collagen	
			340% increase in GAG	
bFGF	10, 100 ng/mL	Pig	128% increase in collagen	[327]
IGF-1	10, 100 ng/mL	Pig	300% increase in collagen	[327]
TGF- β3	5 ng/mL	Pig	Maintained cellularity	[331]
			300% increase in collagen	
			80% increase in GAG	
Combinations of:				
TGF- β1	5, 30 ng/mL	Pig	All growth factor combinations	[4]
IGF-1	10, 100 ng/mL		enhanced construct cellularity and	
bFGF	10, 100 ng/mL		viability relative to controls.	

in matrix structure and mechanical properties. Tissue engineers seek to recreate these forces *in vitro* by using devices which simulate the *in situ* mechanical environment.

The only mechanical stimulation that has been experimentally applied to TMJ disc cells is hydrostatic pressure, when Almarza and Athanasiou [18] demonstrated that static loading at 10 MPa was most beneficial to biosynthesis while cyclic loading was found to be detrimental. This finding was surprising since the disc is assumed to be subjected to cyclic hydrostatic loading *in situ*. Hydrostatic pressure is transmitted through the fluid surrounding tissue. Because water is nearly incompressible at physiological pressures, this loading does not cause an initial change in tissue volume. Instead, the increased fluid pressure upsets the balance between negatively charged GAGs and the water molecules in the matrix, forcing a gradual release of fluid to the synovium. This explains the effect hydrostatic pressure can have on nutrient diffusion, and may help explain why static pressure is beneficial to tissue engineered constructs [359]. There is research that suggests that receptors on the surface of cartilage cells, namely the NA/K, Na/K/2Cl, and Na/H pumps, change conformation and thereby alter intracellular ion concentrations in response to hydrostatic pressure [360, 361]. This change may stimulate signal transduction cascades, causing upregulation of ECM related genes, and enhancing matrix production.

In contrast to hydrostatic pressure, direct stimulation physically compresses the tissue. This type of loading occurs in the TMJ disc during chewing or clenching. Clenching forces would limit small molecule diffusion, and many studies testing static loading on articular cartilage constructs have reported adverse effects [362]–[365]. Dynamic stimulation, however, has shown beneficial effects in cartilage tissue engineering [362, 363, 366]. Mauck et al. [366] reported a 45% increase in GAG and a 37% increase in collagen deposition in response to 10% applied at 1 Hz, and Buschmann et al. [363] reported similar results using 3% strain at 1 Hz. A primary reason cited for the positive effects of this treatment is that mass transfer is enhanced relative to static culture. Compression moves fluid out of the tissue, while unloading allows fluid to be drawn back in to the tissue, thus a complete media change is accomplished through repeated cycles. Additionally, hydrostatic pressure builds up in constructs in response to dynamic loading, and shear stresses develop in response to moving fluids. Although cyclic direct compression was beneficial in cartilage tissue engineering, it actually had a deleterious effect with mandibular condylar cartilage cells [367] (see Chapter 5). Given the similarity of behavior observed with condylar cartilage cells and TMJ disc cells, it is possible that cyclic direct compression may not be efficacious for TMJ disc cells. However, in the event that this approach is attempted for TMJ disc cells, or with any cell source for a TMJ application, it is important to make sure that constructs are sufficiently resilient to handle this type of loading, as high amplitudes and frequencies could easily be detrimental to tissue formation. Such studies would need to optimize the frequency, amplitude, duration, and duty cycle of loading.

Bioreactors are meant to enhance the exchange of nutrients and wastes within constructs. Diffusion limitations in static culture can prevent cells in the center of constructs from having access to fresh media leading to death or inviability. As more biomimetic constructs with greater thicknesses and matrix densities are created, this issue will become more important. In addition, it could be desirable to have closer control over the temporal exposure of cytokines than would be allowed in a system which is limited by the rate of diffusion. Lastly, some bioreactors are able to provide a continuous culture environment. Such a setup would significantly reduce the number of manipulations performed by researchers during culture, greatly reducing construct variability and limiting chances for contamination.

A rotating-wall is an example of a bioreactor. In this system, a vertically oriented culture dish is rotated to create fluid-flow and impart a low-level shear to suspended cells or to constructs [368]. Results with its use for cartilage constructs have been positive, showing significant increases in GAG production, collagen deposition, and increases in equilibrium modulus relative to static controls [369]–[371]. This bioreactor is the only one that has been used for culture of TMJ disc cells, though it was found to have mixed effects [19]. The authors speculated that the shearing fluid washed portions of the scaffold loose along with attached cells and matrix. The results of this study illustrated the need to temper the level of mechanical perturbation at early stages so not to damage immature constructs, for example by preceding bioreactor culture by a period of static culture. This study aside, a low-shear environment provided by the rotating-wall could be beneficial to early stage constructs by enhancing nutrient exchange, so long as the scaffold and cells can withstand shear forces.

CHAPTER 5

Tissue Engineering of the Mandibular Condyle

5.1   INTRODUCTION

The only TMJ structures to have received attention from the tissue engineering community to date have been the TMJ disc and the mandibular condyle. However, unlike the TMJ disc, mandibular condyle/ramus tissue engineering studies did not appear in the literature until the year 2000. Furthermore, there are fewer tissue engineering studies for the mandibular condyle than for the TMJ disc. The remainder of this chapter highlights a few studies of the cells of the condylar cartilage, and reviews the studies of condylar cartilage tissue engineering. For further reading, there is an in depth review of mandibular condyle tissue engineering [298], a review of cartilage tissue engineering in general as it pertains to the TMJ [372], and a review of nanostructured bioceramics for maxillofacial applications that include the TMJ [373].

5.2   CELLS OF THE MANDIBULAR CONDYLAR CARTILAGE

Takigawa et al. [374] developed a method for harvesting mandibular condylar cartilage cells, whereby a rabbit mandibular condyle and disc were removed as a whole and stored in calcium-free and magnesium-free balanced salt solution (pH 7.4). After the removal of the disc and ligament, the mandibular condylar cartilage was separated and minced, then digested in collagenase solution. The cells obtained through this method include various cell types from the different layers in the mandibular condyle.

Another method for harvesting chondrocytes is to allow the cells from cultured explants to migrate out and grow onto a specific substrate. Subsequently, the cells are released from the substrate and suspended in medium. Tsubai et al. [375] used this method to isolate the fibroblast-like cells from the fibrous zone of a fetal rabbit mandibular condyle. The mandibular condyle was collected and then washed in Hanks' Balanced Salt Solution (HBSS), and the tip of the condyle was allowed to contact with a gelfoam surgical sponge for 1 week. After this period, the gelfoam sponge was treated with collagenase to liberate the cells. The cell suspension was centrifuged, and then the cells were resuspended in minimum essential medium (MEM).

A detailed review of the response of condylar cartilage cells to growth factors is available in the literature [298]. In brief, bFGF at high serum concentration thus far generally appears to be the best stimulator of mandibular condylar cartilage cell proliferation, followed by IGF-I [376]–[378]. However, bFGF may inhibit GAG and collagen biosynthesis and inhibit chondrogenesis [378, 379].

IGF-I appears to be a potent promoter of cell proliferation and biosynthesis, especially with regard to GAG production [378], [380]–[382]. TGF-β also appears to be able to induce biosynthesis significantly [376, 378, 383], although there are unresolved inconsistencies between studies on the effect of serum concentration in TGF-β treated medium on cell proliferation. Finally, EGF is a potent inducer of proliferation in fibroblast-like cells isolated from the fibrous zone [375].

Although bFGF and IGF-I may appear to be leading candidates for treatment of cells derived from condylar cartilage, in all likelihood it will be cells from another location that will be employed in a tissue engineering strategy, such as cells from cartilage located elsewhere in the body or stem cells [302, 384], in which case a different growth factor strategy may be necessary. The literature is replete with studies of growth factor effects on various stem cells and on chondrocytes, and it is expected that future applications with mandibular condylar cartilage tissue engineering will benefit from incorporating strategies specific to their cell source gleaned from the literature.

5.3   MANDIBULAR CONDYLE TISSUE ENGINEERING STUDIES

The primary contributions to the mandibular condyle tissue engineering literature have been from the groups of Hollister, Mao, and Detamore. Hollister and colleagues [385] developed a strategy for producing patient-specific condyle-shaped scaffolds based on computed tomography and/or magnetic resonance images dating back to 2000. Their group has employed solid free-form fabrication (creating scaffolds layer by layer) to control the overall shape and internal architecture of their scaffolds, offering precise control over pore size, porosity, permeability, and mechanical integrity (Figure 5.1). Using this method, they have engineered cylindrical osteochondral constructs [24, 25] and condyle/ramus-shaped bone constructs [27] using materials such as hydroxyapatite, polylactic acid, and polycaprolactone and mature cell sources (fibroblasts with bone morphogenetic protein-7 gene inserted and/or chondrocytes). *In vivo* studies via subcutaneous implantation in mice collectively demonstrated substantial bone ingrowth and glycosaminoglycan formation [24, 25, 27, 386]. These studies advanced to a TMJ reconstruction study, using a selective laser sintering (SLS) method (specific type of solid free-form fabrication) to fabricate a PCL condyle/ramus scaffold for implantation into the TMJs of 6 to 8 month old Yucatan minipig [387]. The condylar head of the scaffolds were packed with autologous iliac crest bone marrow, secured to the mandible using miniplates and screws, and evaluated after 1 and 3 months. Compared to controls, there was an increase in regenerated bone volume, and there was evidence of cartilage-like tissue as well.

Mao's group [21]–[23] has taken another approach, encapsulating marrow-derived mesenchymal stem cells in a polyethylene glycol diacrylate hydrogel to create stratified bone and cartilage layers in the shape of a human condyle (Figure 5.2). After 12 weeks of subcutaneous implantation, it was shown that osteopontin, osteonectin, and collagen I were localized in the osteogenic layer and collagen II and glycosaminoglycans were localized in the chondrogenic layer [21].

Detamore's group has also taken a different approach, focusing primarily on the cell source [302, 335, 384]. In one series of studies, porcine mandibular condylar cartilage cells were

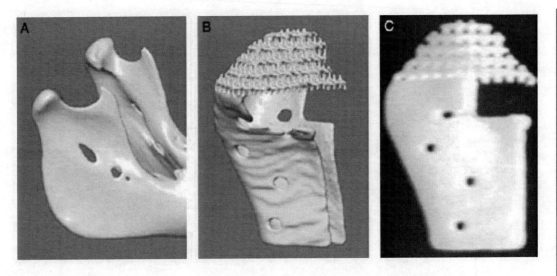

Figure 5.1: Image-based design of patient-specific scaffold. (A) A CT image was taken of the patient's mandible, and then combined with specified microarchitecture to create (B) the design of the implant. This design was fed into a solid free-form fabrication process to create a biodegradable polycaprolactone scaffold with a shape specific to the patient. (Obtained with permission from Schek et al., Orthod Craniofac Res, 2005 [24].)

compared side-by-side with porcine chondrocytes from ankle cartilage in both monolayer [335] and on 3-D scaffolds [302]. In monolayer, the condylar cartilage cells experienced a faster growth rate in terms of proliferation, but the hyaline cartilage cells produced tremendously more extracellular matrix. When compared on PGA scaffolds [302], the condylar cartilage cells were outperformed in matrix synthesis, with hyaline cartilage cells producing amounts up to an order of magnitude higher, with a much larger presence of collagen II relative to collagen I. In an earlier study, porcine condylar cartilage cells were compared with human umbilical cord mesenchymal stromal cells, and the umbilical cord cells were observed to divide much faster and produce significantly more matrix [384].

Beyond the three aforementioned groups, an assortment of different approaches have been employed, most of which were *in vivo* studies using only histology and/or imaging to validate engineered constructs. Two studies from a single group molded coral into the shape of a human condyle and seeded them with mesenchymal stem cells, then implanted them either with BMP-2 in mice to demonstrate osteogenesis [388] or under blood vessels in rabbits to demonstrate construct vascularization [389]. Another approach was to implant poly(lactic-co-glycolic acid) (PLGA)-based constructs with growth factors in rat mandibular defects, which demonstrated the efficacy of TGF-β1 and IGF-I [390] and the lack of efficacy of BMP-2 [118].

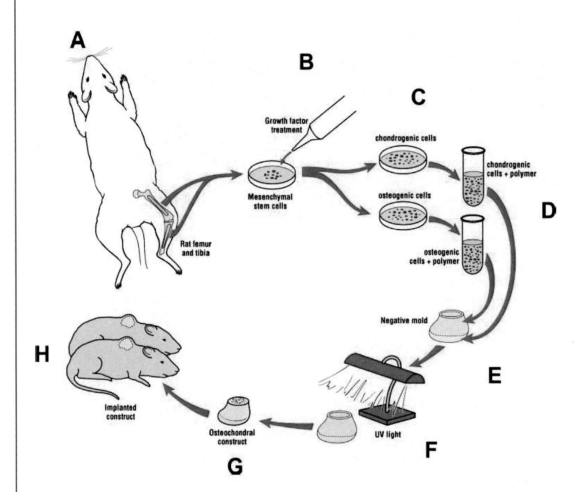

Figure 5.2: Condyle-shaped scaffold. (A) Mesenchymal stem cells (MSCs) are harvested, then (B) expanded and (C) treated with either chondrogenic medium or osteogenic medium. (D) Separate PEG-hydrogel suspensions of MSC-derived chondrogenic and osteogenic cells, with (E) the chondrogenic cell suspension loaded in the negative mold (based on a human cadaver condyle mold) first and (F) photopolymerized. The osteogenic cell suspension was then loaded on top and photopolymerized as well. (G) The fabricated osteochondral constructs were then (H) implanted subcutaneously in immunodeficient mice. (Obtained with permission from Alhadlaq et al., Ann Biomed Eng, 2004 [22].)

In another approach, osteoblasts were seeded into condyle-shaped polyglycolic acid/polylactic acid scaffolds, and chondrocytes were then painted on the surface, and positive histological observations were made following implantation in mice [391]. Positive histological results were also observed in a related study, where porcine mesenchymal stem cells were seeded in condyle-shaped PLGA scaffolds and cultured under osteogenic conditions in a custom-built rotating bioreactor [392].

Studies to date have demonstrated the ability to apply different strategies to create shape-specific scaffolds, have explored different cell sources, and looked at various bioactive signaling strategies. In addition, the response of condylar cartilage cells to dynamic mechanical stimulation in a 3-D environment has also been explored [367]. The next major step for mandibular condyle/ramus tissue engineering will be demonstrating long-term *in vivo* efficacy with osteochondral condyle/ramus replacements in larger animals such as the pig.

CHAPTER 6

Current Perspectives

6.1 CELL SOURCES FOR TISSUE ENGINEERING OF CARTILAGE

6.1.1 PRIMARY CELLS

While previous work using TMJ cells has elucidated their *in vitro* behavior for the purposes of tissue engineering, a clinical solution will likely not involve these cells. A clinically feasible cell source should be abundant, healthy, and leave little donor site morbidity. Selection of an alternative source must also consider the functionality of the cells. Previous characterization data guide this selection. Phenotypic determination of TMJ cartilage as tissues functioning between fibrous tissue and hyaline articular cartilage, as noted in Chapters 2 and 3, indicates the need for fibrochondrocytic cells [242] for TMJ cartilage regeneration. Specifically, the cells should produce tissue containing collagen type I, type II, and proteoglycans, such as aggrecan and decorin, and should support both tensile and compressive loads. Sources of differentiated adult cells other than those from the TMJ could be promising candidates. For example, dermal fibroblasts (DFs) have shown chondrogenic potential despite being inherently fibrous in nature [393, 394]. Similar to articular cartilage, costal cartilage contains collagen type II and GAGs while also containing collagen type I (with a collagen ratio of 5:1 type II to type I in mature adults), suggesting its potential to function as fibrocartilage [395]. Indeed, rib tissue is frequently used in mandibular reconstruction [396]. In addition to its functional potential in TMJ tissue engineering, it is easy to obtain rib tissue and skin biopsies from most adults. These cells are more abundant than TMJ disc and mandibular condylar cartilage cells, rendering them more clinically feasible.

Costal chondrocyte constructs offer several other advantages over TMJ cells that relate directly to their clinical feasibility. Costal cartilage can be obtained from almost any patient with a minimally invasive harvest technique that leaves limited tissue morbidity or other complications [397]. While costal cartilage is a relatively acellular tissue [398], the protocol could be optimized to limit the amount of needed tissue, for example, by expanding the cells before construct formation. Perhaps the most compelling argument for seeking cell sources outside the TMJ is the inherent limitations associated with harvesting autologous TMJ cells from a TMJ patient. Specifically, TMJ cells are scarce, difficult to harvest, and likely diseased in any patient interested in a tissue engineered disc, not to mention that harvest of cells from a previously healthy contralateral TMJ may result in an iatrogenic TMJ disorder.

There is evidence in the literature that supports the use of cells from cartilage sources other than from the TMJ, as described in Chapters 4 and 5. For example, costal chondrocyte constructs produced almost 40 times more collagen and 800 times more glycosaminoglycans than did TMJ disc cell constructs in a scaffoldless approach [1]. With a relatively high number of cells, high ECM production, and capacity to create a replacement tissue of clinically relevant size, the costal cartilage constructs appear able to function as a source of primary cells in a TMJ disc replacement, particularly with this scaffoldless method. Independent studies comparing hyaline cartilage cells with mandibular condylar cartilage cells similarly concluded that the hyaline cartilage cells drastically outperformed the TMJ cells both in monolayer and in 3-D cultures [302, 335].

While using the costal cartilage tissue without *in vitro* manipulation is appealing, previous work with the tissue illustrates the complications that may arise, like tissue overgrowth [399, 400]. This, and concerns about calcification, can likely be addressed through the controlled *in vitro* environment used in this tissue engineering approach. By influencing growth conditions and applied stimuli, constructs can be engineered to have the appropriate dimensions, mechanical and biochemical properties, and, after examining the integrative capacities of such engineered neotissue at different maturities, may even be more readily integrated back into the joint than costal cartilage tissue.

6.1.2   STEM CELLS

Most tissue engineering strategies for the TMJ disc have used primary cells though, increasingly, there is a shift toward stem cells. In contrast, mandibular condylar cartilage studies have predominantly used stem cells. The use of stem cells is based on the fact that in practice there is a lack of sufficient autologous healthy tissue to provide enough cells for a tissue engineered construct. Moreover, the goal of taking only a small biopsy of native tissue and expanding those cells to reach the needed number has been confounded by issues of dedifferentiation, low synthetic capacity, and limited expansion [401]–[404]. These issues are even more pronounced in fibrocartilage compared with hyaline cartilage, as fibrochondrocytes *in vitro* show inferior matrix production compared with chondrocytes [302, 335, 405, 406].

Toward a goal of tissue engineering fibrocartilages, such as the TMJ disc and condylar cartilage, adult, extra-embryonic, and embryonic stem cells may have the capacity to overcome these issues, but they also bring their own challenges. One of the biggest challenges is differentiating the cells. A common treatment in many differentiation studies is the use of serum-free or low-serum "chondrogenic" medium containing insulin, ascorbic acid, and dexamethasone [407]–[409], typically with the addition of a transforming growth factor (TGF). For example, in human embryonic stem cell (hESC) studies, BMP-2 and TGF-β1 have been studied for their efficacy in inducing chondrogenic differentiation [410]–[414]. However, caution should be exercised in the use of dexamethasone and BMP-2 for chondrogenesis, as they are both potent inducers of osteogenesis as well. An additional component of differentiation with ESCs has been the microenvironment for differentiation. Differentiation of embryoid bodies (EBs) can occur in suspension, on a 2-D surface, or a 3-D scaffold such as a hydrogel or polymer scaffold. This microenvironment can also include the presence of other cell types for the purpose of differentiation. Differentiation time prior to use in a tissue engineering strategy is another factor that must be considered. Time frames as short as 8 days have been used [411], whereas Khoo et al. [415] found that hESCs spontaneously differentiated down a cartilaginous lineage after 60 days. Although there is a wide array of studies examining each of these components with adult stem cells [416, 417], the field of TMJ tissue engineering is just beginning with hESCs.

To date, three classes of stem cells have been employed in TMJ tissue engineering. Adult marrow-derived mesenchymal stem cells [21]–[23], [387] and human umbilical cord mesenchymal stromal cells [384] have been utilized in condylar cartilage tissue engineering, and ESCs have been studied for TMJ disc tissue engineering [418].

In one study, the effect of differentiation time on the functional fibrochondrogenic differentiation of two different human embryonic stem cell lines, H9 and BG01V, was examined [419]. Using a chondrogenic medium containing 1% serum, dexamethasone, ITS, and ascorbic acid, EBs were differentiated for 1, 3, or 6 weeks, spanning the differentiation times used in prior studies of cartilaginous differentiation. The resulting cells were then cultured at high density in agarose molds (scaffoldless) for 4 weeks to create neotissue constructs. Matrix produced was fibrocartilaginous, containing GAGs and collagen types I, II, and VI for all combinations. Both 3 and 6 week differentiation timelines produced homogeneous constructs, with matrix composition varying greatly with cell line and differentiation time. One week of differentiation resulted in small constructs with poor structural integrity that were not mechanically testable. The compressive stiffness did not vary significantly with either differentiation time or cell line. In contrast, the tensile properties were far greater in the H9 groups (1.5–1.9 MPa) than in the BG01V groups (32–80 kPa).

6.2   THE JOINT CAPSULE AND THE SYNOVIUM

Other cartilaginous and fibrous components of the joint, the joint capsule and the synovium, have not garnered much interest from tissue engineers, as disease of these tissues may not be as prevalent or apparent. However, the community of researchers would likely benefit from biochemical and biomechanical characterization of these tissues, as they would provide a complete description of the TMJ. In addition, a tissue engineered disc or condyle would interact with or be attached to these structures, further necessitating an understanding of their mechanical behavior. However, those other tissues are likely not of interest to surgeons in the early stages of clinical application, although in the long-term they may be incorporated as "polishing" features once tissue engineering of the two primary components—disc and condyle/ramus—is achieved.

The fibrous joint capsule, which encloses the joint [28], is reinforced laterally by the temporomandibular (lateral) ligament, and posteriorly by retrodiscal tissue or posterior attachments. As described in Chapter 1, attachments between the capsule and disc produce closed superior and inferior joint spaces (Figure 1.2). The capsule and ligament (Figure 2.4) are highly innervated structures, containing a significant number of receptors that are capable of detecting stretch and pressure. Pacinian corpuscles, Ruffini nerve endings, Golgi tendon bodies, and free nerve endings have all been identified in the joint capsule [420]. These receptors provide important proprioceptive signals that guide the position of the mandible through neural relays with the muscles of mastication. While joint sensation is commonly ascribed to the auriculotemporal nerve, the role of other neurological mechanisms governing joint motion and mandibular position are not well understood. This lack of characterization contributes to the morbidity associated with reconstructive procedures.

The inner surfaces of the capsule are lined by the synovial membrane, a specialized structure containing cells and vessels responsible for both the phagocytosis of foreign particles and potentially pathological organisms and the production of synovial fluid [28]. Synovial fluid serves two principal functions within a joint: lubrication and nutrient transmission. The lubricating action of synovial fluid is complex in itself and involves the interaction of multiple proteins [421]. Synovial fluid also acts as a medium for the transmission of nutrients and the removal of metabolic waste from the cells present within the joint. As a dialysate of plasma, it contains all the components of plasma with the exception of large coagulation proteins. This composition suggests that synovial fluid is capable of performing most of the physiological functions of blood and is essential to the viability of joint structures. In the future, tissue engineering products aimed at reconstruction of the TMJ or its components must be coupled with efforts that restore the functions of the synovium.

6.3   DESIGN STANDARDS FOR TISSUE ENGINEERING

It is generally agreed that the primary clinical problems for the TMJ are pain, obstruction of mouth opening, and joint degeneration (due to osteoarthrosis, rheumatoid arthritis, trauma, abnormal loading, etc.). A recent conference group on TMJ bioengineering discussed how to design approaches for functional tissue engineering to address TMJ morbidity [136]. The participants thought that animal models need to be developed to reliably mimic the process of degeneration in the TMJ. Furthermore, a complete characterization of the mechanical, structural, and biochemical properties of the TMJ tissues needs to be performed. More importantly, outcome measures of the tissue engineering approaches should include functional assessment including normalization of pain, range of motion, chewing capacity, bite force, and so on.

The main design standards important for tissue engineering a functional TMJ are proper geometry, biomechanics, and biocompatibility. The geometry of the TMJ tissues has a central role in allowing for smooth joint movement and stabilization. The TMJ disc rests in a specific place between the condyle and fossa to allow for a smooth motion between these two incongruent structures. Furthermore, the shape of the condyle mimics that of the disc; thus the shape and size of tissue engineered constructs should match those of the native disc and condyle to best restore function. The anisotropic material behavior of the TMJ disc and mandibular condyle cartilage in tension, compression, and shear allows for dynamic load bearing and distribution and is imparted to the tissue through the organization of matrix molecules. Engineered TMJ tissues must also withstand these loading patterns, either by organized matrix deposition or other means. For example, in the TMJ disc, circumferential tensile properties for the engineered tissue must be higher than in the intermediate zone, and compressive properties must be higher in the center of the disc than in the periphery. Having mechanical properties regionally similar to native values will ensure that the construct is not destroyed upon implantation. This is especially important if the engineered tissue is used to fill a defect site, in which case mechanical similarity will ensure a normal distribution of load.

Creating a biomechanically robust tissue is also advantageous for surgical implantation. Fixation methods involving sutures place great amounts of local stress on the tissue. As it is known that the TMJ disc relies heavily on capsular attachments for anchoring within the joint, it is imperative that a replacement tissue is able to withstand these fixation stresses in addition to loading stresses.

The safety of an implantable TMJ tissue replacement is not only linked to its function within the joint, but also to its immune response. Biocompatibility is a primary concern for tissue engineering of TMJ tissue analogues as this attribute can increase safety, which is highly important for eventual clinical approval. Increasing the biocompatibility of the engineered tissue by using natural scaffolds or scaffolds with non-toxic degradation products, or using autologous cells can reduce the likelihood of an immune reaction in the body.

6.4   ASSESSMENTS OF TISSUE ENGINEERED CONSTRUCTS

Methods to functionally evaluate engineered TMJ tissue include histological assessment, biochemical assays, molecular biology assays (real time RT-PCR), and mechanical tests (as described in Chapter 1). Together, these measurements allow for a thorough comparison of tissue engineering constructs to native tissue. Several of these methods are described in this section.

Extracellular matrix distribution – Histology: For qualitative characterization of the distribution of newly produced ECM, histology is often used. Tissue slides are stained for different ECM or cellular components. For example, a hematoxylin and eosin (H&E) stain, used to visualize cells, will stain the ECM pink and the cell nuclei purple. Picrosirius red staining is used to visualize collagen distribution, staining collagen red. A modified Movat stain can also be used to visualize collagen bundles and GAG regions with different colors. Alternately, GAGs can be stained using either an alcian blue or safranin-O stain.

Biochemical organization – Immunohistochemistry: To visualize the distributions of specific proteins, such as collagen type I, collagen type II, elastin, and GAGs such as chondroitin-4-sulfate, chondroitin-6-sulfate, keratan sulfate, dermatan sulfate and hyaluronic acid, immunohistochemistry is used. The fibrocartilage or tissue engineering construct is first frozen and sections are taken. Frozen sections are preferred since paraffin prevents binding of antibodies. Immunostaining consists of exposing the sample to a primary antibody (preferably monoclonal) to specifically recognize the protein of interest. Then, biotinylated secondary antibodies are added that recognize the primary antibody. Generally, the primary antibody comes from a different species than the sample, and the secondary antibody comes from a third species. Finally, a complex is added to bind to the antibodies and allow color change, and a coloring agent is added for visualization.

Biochemical content – Biochemistry: Biochemical analyses are performed to quantify the matrix content of tissue engineering constructs. Constructs are lyophilized and the dry weight of each scaffold is determined. Water content is determined by comparison to the wet weight taken prior to lyophilization. Dry constructs are then digested with a strong enzyme, such as papain. Following digestion, several biochemical assays can be performed.

DNA content is quantified by reaction with a reagent (such as PicoGreen) and compared to standards included by the supplier. Cellularity can be determined using a cell/DNA ratio specific to the source species. Total amount of GAG is determined by a dimethylmethylene blue colorimetric assay, with standards provided by the manufacturer. The total collagen content is determined by a hydroxyproline assay [423] where collagen standards can be used.

Biochemical content – ELISA: Enzyme-linked immunosorbent assays (ELISAs) can be used to quantify specific proteins. Dried specimens are solubilized in gentle digests that break up the tissue but do not cleave the protein of interest, such as pepsin and elastase. In a sandwich ELISA, a capture antibody is adsorbed to the surface of a polystyrene multi-well plate, then samples and standards are attached. Next, a biotinylated detection antibody is attached to the sample, and an enzyme is attached to the detection antibody. After addition of a substrate (such as TMB), a color change occurs which is proportional the concentration of the protein in solution. Kits can be purchased to perform assessments for specific proteins and other species.

Real-time RT-PCR – RNA isolation and PCR: To perform gene expression analysis, RNA must be isolated, Commercial kits are available which isolate RNA from cells in monolayer and in 3-D culture. PCR reads complementary DNA (cDNA), therefore RNA must be made by reaction with reverse transcriptase (RT). The cDNA obtained needs to be amplified to determine the abundance of specific genes. A PCR cycler is used to amplify the gene of interest for abundance detection. For each gene, a forward primer, reverse primer, and gene specific probe can be used. The PCR cycler steps through several cycles of three different temperatures to separate the strands, bind the primers to the correct sequences, and expand the DNA sequence (amplification). During the last point of each cycle the fluorescence is measured for each gene of interest and recorded in real time.

Real-time RT-PCR – Abundance: Gene expression for all the sample groups can be normalized by RNA concentration into the RT reaction. This allows for the calculation of an abundance value (A) calculated from the take-off cycle (C_t) for each gene of interest and the efficiency (E) for that gene. The C_t is the cycle number in which the gene began to be amplified, and the E for each reaction is obtained from a standard curve. Thus, the abundance of each gene is given by:

$$A_{\text{gene}} = \frac{1}{\left(1 + E_{\text{gene}}\right)^{C_{t,\text{gene}}}} \tag{1}$$

The data are then represented by fold differences by comparing the abundance of each target gene of the experimental group to the average value of the control group.

6.5   DIRECTIONS TO IMPROVE PATIENT OUTCOMES

The structure/function relationships described in this book provide a framework for development of solutions to the problems of TMD. Though the structures of the TMJ are not as well characterized as other musculoskeletal tissues, increasing interest in this field bodes well for prospects of developing new and viable solutions to tackle the complex problems of TMJ pathophysiology. In addition, the development of alternative cell sources has greatly expanded the possibilities for a creation of a wide variety of fibrocartilages. The future undoubtedly holds promise for the successful development of tissue engineering solutions to the largely untreated problems associated with TMD.

Whether or not engineered TMJ tissue will perform well *in vivo* may depend on many different factors, including biochemical and biomechanical properties of the engineered neotissue, as well as the presence of inflammation. Not only do laboratories engaged in tissue engineering need standards to evaluate the functionality of their work, but regulatory agencies must likewise determine the type of assessments required for approval of such products.

These complex issues may require a combination of approaches, including gene and cell therapies, as well as biologic scaffolds. Indeed, functional tissue engineering has generated many exciting developments. To translate the knowledge gained about a particular gene, protein, or cell to a clinical application will require expertise from many disciplines to work in a seamless fashion. One of the roles of biomedical engineers within this framework would be to help link interactions of the functions of molecules to cells, cells to tissues, tissues to organs, and organs to body. As biologists, biomedical engineers, clinicians, as well as experts from other disciplines, work together, they will undoubtedly develop better therapies that will allow healing of the injured cartilages with neotissue possessing properties closer to those of normal tissues. Multidisciplinary efforts of such a team-based approach will not only allow for the elucidation of normal and pathologic physiologies, but will also result in new tissue engineering developments that, together, will bring a bright future toward tackling TMJ pathologies and improving patient outcomes.

Bibliography

[1] Johns DE, Wong ME, Athanasiou KA. Clinically relevant cell sources for TMJ disc engineering. J Dent Res 2008 Jun;87(6):548-552. DOI: 10.1177/154405910808700609

[2] Almarza AJ, Athanasiou KA. Seeding techniques and scaffolding choice for tissue engineering of the temporomandibular joint disk. Tissue Eng 2004 Nov-Dec;10(11-12):1787-1795. DOI: 10.1089/ten.2004.10.1787

[3] Almarza AJ, Athanasiou KA. Effects of initial cell seeding density for the tissue engineering of the temporomandibular joint disc. Ann Biomed Eng 2005 Jul;33(7):943-950. DOI: 10.1007/s10439-005-3311-8

[4] Almarza AJ, Athanasiou KA. Evaluation of three growth factors in combinations of two for temporomandibular joint disc tissue engineering. Arch Oral Biol 2006 Mar;51(3):215-221. DOI: 10.1016/j.archoralbio.2005.07.002

[5] Hu JC, Athanasiou KA. A self-assembling process in articular cartilage tissue engineering. Tissue Eng 2006 Apr;12(4):969-979. DOI: 10.1089/ten.2006.12.969

[6] Allen KD, Athanasiou KA. Tissue Engineering of the TMJ disc: a review. Tissue Eng 2006 May;12(5):1183-1196. DOI: 10.1089/ten.2006.12.1183

[7] Detamore MS, Athanasiou KA. Structure and function of the temporomandibular joint disc: implications for tissue engineering. J Oral Maxillofac Surg 2003 Apr;61(4):494-506. DOI: 10.1053/joms.2003.50096

[8] Thomas M, Grande D, Haug RH. Development of an in vitro temporomandibular joint cartilage analog. J Oral Maxillofac Surg 1991 Aug;49(8):854-856; discussion 857. DOI: 10.1016/0278-2391(91)90015-E

[9] Puelacher WC, Wisser J, Vacanti CA, Ferraro NF, Jaramillo D, Vacanti JP. Temporomandibular joint disc replacement made by tissue-engineered growth of cartilage. J Oral Maxillofac Surg 1994;52(11):1172-1177.

[10] Girdler NM. In vitro synthesis and characterization of a cartilaginous meniscus grown from isolated temporomandibular chondroprogenitor cells. Scand J Rheumatol 1998;27(6):446-453.

[11] Glowacki J. Engineered cartilage, bone, joints, and menisci. Potential for temporomandibular joint reconstruction. Cells Tissues Organs 2001;169(3):302-308.

[12] Poshusta AK, Anseth KS. Photopolymerized biomaterials for application in the temporomandibular joint. Cells Tissues Organs 2001;169(3):272-278.

[13] Singh M, Berkland C, Detamore MS. Strategies and applications for incorporating physical and chemical signal gradients in tissue engineering. Tissue Eng Part B Rev 2008 Dec;14(4):341-366. DOI: 10.1089/ten.teb.2008.0304

[14] Almarza AJ, Athanasiou KA. Evaluation of three growth factors in combinations of two for TMJ disc tissue engineering. Archives of Oral Biology 2005:Submitted.

[15] Detamore MS, Athanasiou KA. Effects of growth factors on temporomandibular joint disc cells. Arch Oral Biol 2004 Jul;49(7):577-583. DOI: 10.1016/j.archoralbio.2004.01.015

[16] Bean AC, Almarza AJ, Athanasiou KA. Effects of ascorbic acid concentration on the tissue engineering of the temporomandibular joint disc. Proc Inst Mech Eng [H] 2006 Apr;220(3):439-447. DOI: 10.1243/09544119JEIM51

[17] Allen KD, Athanasiou KA. Effect of passage and topography on gene expression of temporomandibular joint disc cells. Tissue Eng 2007 Jan;13(1):101-110. DOI: 10.1089/ten.2006.0094

[18] Almarza AJ, Athanasiou KA. Effects of hydrostatic pressure on TMJ disc cells. Tissue Eng 2006 May;12(5):1285-1294. DOI: 10.1089/ten.2006.12.1285

[19] Detamore MS, Athanasiou KA. Use of a rotating bioreactor toward tissue engineering the temporomandibular joint disc. Tissue Eng 2005 Jul-Aug;11(7-8):1188-1197. DOI: 10.1089/ten.2005.11.1188

[20] Hanaoka K, Tanaka E, Takata T, Miyauchi M, Aoyama J, Kawai N, et al. Platelet-derived growth factor enhances proliferation and matrix synthesis of temporomandibular joint disc-derived cells. Angle Orthod 2006 May;76(3):486-492.

[21] Alhadlaq A, Mao JJ. Tissue-engineered osteochondral constructs in the shape of an articular condyle. J Bone Joint Surg Am 2005 May;87(5):936-944. DOI: 10.2106/JBJS.D.02104

[22] Alhadlaq A, Elisseeff JH, Hong L, Williams CG, Caplan AI, Sharma B, et al. Adult stem cell driven genesis of human-shaped articular condyle. Ann Biomed Eng 2004 Jul;32(7):911-9 DOI: 10.1023/B:ABME.0000032454.53116.ee

[23] 23. Alhadlaq A, Mao JJ. Tissue-engineered neogenesis of human-shaped mandibular condyle from rat mesenchymal stem cells. J Dent Res 2003 Dec;82(12):951-956. DOI: 10.1177/154405910308201203

[24] Schek RM, Taboas JM, Hollister SJ, Krebsbach PH. Tissue engineering osteochondral implants for temporomandibular joint repair. Orthod Craniofac Res 2005 Nov;8(4):313-319. DOI: 10.1111/j.1601-6343.2005.00354.x

[25] Schek RM, Taboas JM, Segvich SJ, Hollister SJ, Krebsbach PH. Engineered osteochondral grafts using biphasic composite solid free-form fabricated scaffolds. Tissue Eng 2004 Sep-Oct;10(9-10):1376-1385. DOI: 10.1089/ten.2004.10.1376

[26] Hollister SJ, Lin CY, Saito E, Schek RD, Taboas JM, Williams JM, et al. Engineering craniofacial scaffolds. Orthod Craniofac Res 2005 Aug;8(3):162-173. DOI: 10.1111/j.1601-6343.2005.00329.x

[27] Williams JM, Adewunmi A, Schek RM, Flanagan CL, Krebsbach PH, Feinberg SE, et al. Bone tissue engineering using polycaprolactone scaffolds fabricated via selective laser sintering. Biomaterials 2005 Aug;26(23):4817-4827. DOI: 10.1016/j.biomaterials.2004.11.057

[28] Wong ME, Allen KD, Athanasiou KA. Tissue Engineering of the Temporomandibular Joint. In: Bronzino JD, editor. Tissue Engineering and Artificial Organs. Boca Raton, FL: CRC Press, 2006.

[29] Dolwick MF. The temporomandibular joint: normal and abnormal anatomy. In: Helms CA, Katzberg RW, Dolwick MF, editors. Internal Derangements of the Temporomandibular Joint. San Francisco, CA: Radiology Research and Education Foundation, 1983. p. 1-14.

[30] Rees LA. The structure and function of the mandibular joint. Br Dent J 1954 March 16;96(6):125-133.

[31] Gillbe GV. The function of the disc of the temporomandibular joint. J Prosthet Dent 1975 Feb;33(2):196-204. DOI: 10.1016/S0022-3913(75)80110-7

[32] Gallo LM, Nickel JC, Iwasaki LR, Palla S. Stress-field translation in the healthy human temporomandibular joint. J Dent Res 2000 Oct;79(10):1740-1746. DOI: 10.1177/00220345000790100201

[33] Ten Cate AR. Oral histology : development, structure, and function. 5th ed. St. Louis: Mosby, 1998

[34] Solberg WK, Woo MW, Houston JB. Prevalence of mandibular dysfunction in young adults. J Am Dent Assoc 1979;98(1):25-34.

[35] Gray RJM, Davies SJ, Quayle AA. Temporomandibular Disorders: A Clinical Approach. London: British Dental Association, 1995

[36] Carlsson GE, LeResche L. Epidemiology of temporomandibular disorders. In: Sessle BJ, Bryant P, Dionne R, editors. Temporomandibular disorders and related pain conditions. Seattle: IASP Press, 1995. p. 497-506.

[37] Carlsson GE. Epidemiology and treatment need for temporomandibular disorders. J Orofac Pain 1999 Fall;13(4):232-237.

[38] Mejersjo C, Hollender L. Radiography of the temporomandibular joint in female patients with TMJ pain or dysfunction. A seven year follow-up. Acta Radiol Diagn (Stockh) 1984;25(3):169-176.

[39] Brooks SL, Westesson PL, Eriksson L, Hansson LG, Barsotti JB. Prevalence of osseous changes in the temporomandibular joint of asymptomatic persons without internal derangement. Oral Surg Oral Med Oral Pathol 1992 Jan;73(1):118-122. DOI: 10.1016/0030-4220(92)90168-P

[40] Zarb GA, Carlsson GE. Temporomandibular disorders: osteoarthritis. J Orofac Pain 1999 Fall;13(4):295-306.

[41] Wilkes CH. Internal derangements of the temporomandibular joint. Pathological variations. Arch Otolaryngol Head Neck Surg 1989 Apr;115(4):469-477.

[42] Tanaka E, Detamore MS, Mercuri LG. Degenerative disorders of the temporomandibular joint: etiology, diagnosis, and treatment. J Dent Res 2008 Apr;87(4):296-307. DOI: 10.1177/154405910808700406

[43] Takano Y, Moriwake Y, Tohno Y, Minami T, Tohno S, Utsumi M, et al. Age-related changes of elements in the human articular disk of the temporomandibular joint. Biol Trace Elem Res 1999 Mar;67(3):269-276. DOI: 10.1007/BF02784426

[44] Jibiki M, Shimoda S, Nakagawa Y, Kawasaki K, Asada K, Ishibashi K. Calcifications of the disc of the temporomandibular joint. J Oral Pathol Med 1999 Oct;28(9):413-419.

[45] Tanaka E, Sasaki A, Tahmina K, Yamaguchi K, Mori Y, Tanne K. Mechanical properties of human articular disk and its influence on TMJ loading studied with the finite element method. J Oral Rehabil 2001 Mar;28(3):273-279. DOI: 10.1111/j.1365-2842.2001.tb01677.x

[46] Holmes MW, Bayliss MT, Muir H. Hyaluronic acid in human articular cartilage. Age-related changes in content and size. Biochem J 1988 Mar 1;250(2):435-441.

[47] Smartt JM, Jr., Low DW, Bartlett SP. The pediatric mandible: I. A primer on growth and development. Plast Reconstr Surg 2005 Jul;116(1):14e-23e. DOI: 10.1097/01.PRS.0000169940.69315.9C

[48] Arnett GW, Milam SB, Gottesman L. Progressive mandibular retrusion-idiopathic condylar resorption. Part II. Am J Orthod Dentofacial Orthop 1996 Aug;110(2):117-127. DOI: 10.1016/S0889-5406(96)70099-9

[49] Arnett GW, Milam SB, Gottesman L. Progressive mandibular retrusion–idiopathic condylar resorption. Part I. Am J Orthod Dentofacial Orthop 1996 Jul;110(1):8-15. DOI: 10.1016/S0889-5406(96)70081-1

[50] Nitzan DW. The process of lubrication impairment and its involvement in temporomandibular joint disc displacement: a theoretical concept. J Oral Maxillofac Surg 2001 Jan;59(1):36-45. DOI: 10.1053/joms.2001.19278

[51] Stegenga B, de Bont LG, Boering G. Osteoarthrosis as the cause of craniomandibular pain and dysfunction: a unifying concept. J Oral Maxillofac Surg 1989 Mar;47(3):249-256. DOI: 10.1016/0278-2391(89)90227-9

[52] Nickel JC, Iwasaki LR, Feely DE, Stormberg KD, Beatty MW. The effect of disc thickness and trauma on disc surface friction in the porcine temporomandibular joint. Arch Oral Biol 2001 Feb;46(2):155-162. DOI: 10.1016/S0003-9969(00)00101-1

[53] Beatty MW, Bruno MJ, Iwasaki LR, Nickel JC. Strain rate dependent orthotropic properties of pristine and impulsively loaded porcine temporomandibular joint disk. J Biomed Mater Res 2001;57(1):25-34.

[54] Beatty MW, Nickel JC, Iwasaki LR, Leiker M. Mechanical response of the porcine temporomandibular joint disc to an impact event and repeated tensile loading. J Orofac Pain 2003 Spring;17(2):160-166.

[55] Gallo LM, Chiaravalloti G, Iwasaki LR, Nickel JC, Palla S. Mechanical work during stress-field translation in the human TMJ. J Dent Res 2006 Nov;85(11):1006-1010. DOI: 10.1177/154405910608501106

[56] Hiraba K, Hibino K, Hiranuma K, Negoro T. EMG activities of two heads of the human lateral pterygoid muscle in relation to mandibular condyle movement and biting force. J Neurophysiol 2000 Apr;83(4):2120-2137.

[57] Murray GM, Phanachet I, Uchida S, Whittle T. The role of the human lateral pterygoid muscle in the control of horizontal jaw movements. J Orofac Pain 2001 Fall;15(4):279-292; discussion 292-305.

[58] Athanasiou KA, Natoli RM. Introduction to continuum biomechanics: Morgan & Claypool, 2008

[59] Beatty MW. Poisson's ratio measurements of the porcine temporomandibular joint disc. The IADR/AADR/CADR 80th General Session; 2002; San Diego; 2002.

[60] Kim KW, Wong ME, Helfrick JF, Thomas JB, Athanasiou KA. Biomechanical tissue characterization of the superior joint space of the porcine temporomandibular joint. Ann Biomed Eng 2003 Sep;31(8):924-930. DOI: 10.1114/1.1591190

[61] Detamore MS, Athanasiou KA. Tensile properties of the porcine temporomandibular joint disc. J Biomech Eng 2003 Aug;125(4):558-565. DOI: 10.1115/1.1589778

[62] Singh M, Detamore MS. Tensile properties of the mandibular condylar cartilage. J Biomech Eng 2008 Feb;130(1):011009. DOI: 10.1115/1.2838062

[63] Snider GR, Lomakin J, Singh M, Gehrke SH, Detamore MS. Regional dynamic tensile properties of the TMJ disc. J Dent Res 2008 Nov;87(11):1053-1057. DOI: 10.1177/154405910808701112

[64] Tanaka E, Aoyama J, Tanaka M, Murata H, Hamada T, Tanne K. Dynamic properties of bovine temporomandibular joint disks change with age. J Dent Res 2002 Sep;81(9):618-622. DOI: 10.1177/154405910208100908

[65] Tanaka E, Aoyama J, Tanaka M, Van Eijden T, Sugiyama M, Hanaoka K, et al. The proteoglycan contents of the temporomandibular joint disc influence its dynamic viscoelastic properties. J Biomed Mater Res A 2003 Jun 1;65(3):386-392. DOI: 10.1002/jbm.a.10496

[66] Tanaka E, del Pozo R, Tanaka M, Aoyama J, Hanaoka K, Nakajima A, et al. Strain-rate effect on the biomechanical response of bovine temporomandibular joint disk under compression. J Biomed Mater Res A 2003 Dec 1;67(3):761-765. DOI: 10.1002/jbm.a.10019

[67] Tanaka E, Hanaoka K, van Eijden T, Tanaka M, Watanabe M, Nishi M, et al. Dynamic shear properties of the temporomandibular joint disc. J Dent Res 2003 Mar;82(3):228-231. DOI: 10.1177/154405910308200315

[68] Tanaka E, Kikuzaki M, Hanaoka K, Tanaka M, Sasaki A, Kawai N, et al. Dynamic compressive properties of porcine temporomandibular joint disc. Eur J Oral Sci 2003 Oct;111(5):434-439. DOI: 10.1034/j.1600-0722.2003.00066.x

[69] Tanaka E, Yamano E, Dalla-Bona DA, Watanabe M, Inubushi T, Shirakura M, et al. Dynamic compressive properties of the mandibular condylar cartilage. J Dent Res 2006 Jun;85(6):571-575. DOI: 10.1177/154405910608500618

[70] Tanaka E, Iwabuchi Y, Rego EB, Koolstra JH, Yamano E, Hasegawa T, et al. Dynamic shear behavior of mandibular condylar cartilage is dependent on testing direction. J Biomech 2008;41(5):1119-1123.

[71] Tanaka E, Rego EB, Iwabuchi Y, Inubushi T, Koolstra JH, van Eijden TM, et al. Biomechanical response of condylar cartilage-on-bone to dynamic shear. J Biomed Mater Res A 2008 Apr;85(1):127-132.

[72] Hylander WL. Experimental analysis of temporomandibular joint reaction force in macaques. Am J Phys Anthropol 1979 Sep;51(3):433-456. DOI: 10.1002/ajpa.1330510317

[73] Hylander WL, Bays R. An in vivo strain-gauge analysis of the squamosal-dentary joint reaction force during mastication and incisal biting in Macaca mulatta and Macaca fascicularis. Arch Oral Biol 1979;24(9):689-697.

[74] Hylander WL. The human mandible: lever or link? Am J Phys Anthropol 1975 Sep;43(2):227-242. DOI: 10.1002/ajpa.1330430209

[75] Throckmorton GS, Dechow PC. In vitro strain measurements in the condylar process of the human mandible. Arch Oral Biol 1994 Oct;39(10):853-867. DOI: 10.1016/0003-9969(94)90017-5

[76] Herring SW, Liu ZJ. Loading of the temporomandibular joint: anatomical and in vivo evidence from the bones. Cells Tissues Organs 2001;169(3):193-200.

[77] Marks L, Teng S, Artun J, Herring S. Reaction strains on the condylar neck during mastication and maximum muscle stimulation in different condylar positions: an experimental study in the miniature pig. J Dent Res 1997 Jul;76(7):1412-1420.

[78] Liu ZJ, Herring SW. Bone surface strains and internal bony pressures at the jaw joint of the miniature pig during masticatory muscle contraction. Arch Oral Biol 2000 Feb;45(2):95-112.

[79] Hohl TH, Tucek WH. Measurement of condylar loading forces by instrumented prosthesis in the baboon. J Maxillofac Surg 1982 Feb;10(1):1-7. DOI: 10.1016/S0301-0503(82)80003-9

[80] Roth TE, Goldberg JS, Behrents RG. Synovial fluid pressure determination in the temporomandibular joint. Oral Surg Oral Med Oral Pathol 1984;57(6):583-588.

[81] Ward DM, Behrents RG, Goldberg JS. Temporomandibular synovial fluid pressure response to altered mandibular positions. Am J Orthod Dentofacial Orthop 1990 Jul;98(1):22-28. DOI: 10.1016/0889-5406(90)70027-A

[82] Nitzan DW. Intraarticular pressure in the functioning human temporomandibular joint and its alteration by uniform elevation of the occlusal plane. J Oral Maxillofac Surg 1994 Jul;52(7):671-679; discussion 679-680. DOI: 10.1016/0278-2391(94)90476-6

[83] Tanaka E, van Eijden T. Biomechanical behavior of the temporomandibular joint disc. Crit Rev Oral Biol Med 2003;14(2):138-150.

[84] Donzelli PS, Gallo LM, Spilker RL, Palla S. Biphasic finite element simulation of the TMJ disc from in vivo kinematic and geometric measurements. J Biomech 2004 Nov;37(11):1787-1791. DOI: 10.1016/j.jbiomech.2004.01.029

[85] Beek M, Koolstra JH, van Ruijven LJ, van Eijden TM. Three-dimensional finite element analysis of the human temporomandibular joint disc. J Biomech 2000;33(3):307-316.

[86] Tanaka E, del Pozo R, Tanaka M, Asai D, Hirose M, Iwabe T, et al. Three-dimensional finite element analysis of human temporomandibular joint with and without disc displacement during jaw opening. Med Eng Phys 2004 Jul;26(6):503-511. DOI: 10.1016/j.medengphy.2004.03.001

[87] Chen J, Xu L. A finite element analysis of the human temporomandibular joint. J Biomech Eng 1994 Nov;116(4):401-407. DOI: 10.1115/1.2895790

[88] DeVocht JW, Goel VK, Zeitler DL, Lew D. A study of the control of disc movement within the temporomandibular joint using the finite element technique. J Oral Maxillofac Surg 1996;54(12):1431-1437; discussion 1437-1438.

[89] DeVocht JW, Goel VK, Zeitler DL, Lew D. A study of the control of disc movement within the temporomandibular joint using the finite element technique. J Oral Maxillofac Surg 1996 Dec;54(12):1431-1437; discussion 1437-1438. DOI: 10.1016/S0278-2391(96)90259-1

[90] Chen J, Akyuz U, Xu L, Pidaparti RM. Stress analysis of the human temporomandibular joint. Med Eng Phys 1998;20(8):565-572.

[91] Beek M, Koolstra JH, van Eijden TM. Human temporomandibular joint disc cartilage as a poroelastic material. Clin Biomech (Bristol, Avon) 2003 Jan;18(1):69-76. DOI: 10.1016/S0268-0033(02)00135-3

[92] Pérez del Palomar A, Doblaré M. The effect of collagen reinforcement in the behaviour of the temporomandibular joint disc. J Biomech 2006;39(6):1075-1085.

[93] Gallo LM. Modeling of temporomandibular joint function using MRI and jaw-tracking technologies–mechanics. Cells Tissues Organs 2005;180(1):54-68.

[94] Palla S, Gallo LM, Gossi D. Dynamic stereometry of the temporomandibular joint. Orthod Craniofac Res 2003;6 Suppl 1:37-47.

[95] Fushima K, Gallo LM, Krebs M, Palla S. Analysis of the TMJ intraarticular space variation: a non-invasive insight during mastication. Med Eng Phys 2003 Apr;25(3):181-190. DOI: 10.1016/S1350-4533(02)00184-4

[96] Gossi DB, Gallo LM, Bahr E, Palla S. Dynamic intra-articular space variation in clicking TMJs. J Dent Res 2004 Jun;83(6):480-484. DOI: 10.1177/154405910408300609

[97] Paige KT, Cima LG, Yaremchuk MJ, Schloo BL, Vacanti JP, Vacanti CA. De novo cartilage generation using calcium alginate-chondrocyte constructs. Plast Reconstr Surg 1996 Jan;97(1):168-178; discussion 179-180. DOI: 10.1097/00006534-199601000-00027

[98] Aigner J, Tegeler J, Hutzler P, Campoccia D, Pavesio A, Hammer C, et al. Cartilage tissue engineering with novel nonwoven structured biomaterial based on hyaluronic acid benzyl ester. J Biomed Mater Res 1998 Nov;42(2):172-181. DOI: 10.1002/(SICI)1097-4636(199811)42:2<172::AID-JBM2>3.0.CO;2-M

[99] Silverman RP, Passaretti D, Huang W, Randolph MA, Yaremchuk MJ. Injectable tissue-engineered cartilage using a fibrin glue polymer. Plast Reconstr Surg 1999 Jun;103(7):1809-1818. DOI: 10.1097/00006534-199906000-00001

[100] Peretti GM, Randolph MA, Villa MT, Buragas MS, Yaremchuk MJ. Cell-based tissue-engineered allogeneic implant for cartilage repair. Tissue Eng 2000 Oct;6(5):567-576. DOI: 10.1089/107632700750022206

[101] Passaretti D, Silverman RP, Huang W, Kirchhoff CH, Ashiku S, Randolph MA, et al. Cultured chondrocytes produce injectable tissue-engineered cartilage in hydrogel polymer. Tissue Eng 2001 Dec;7(6):805-815. DOI: 10.1089/107632701753337744

[102] Kaps C, Bramlage C, Smolian H, Haisch A, Ungethum U, Burmester GR, et al. Bone morphogenetic proteins promote cartilage differentiation and protect engineered artificial cartilage from fibroblast invasion and destruction. Arthritis Rheum 2002 Jan;46(1):149-162. DOI: 10.1002/1529-0131(200201)46:1<149::AID-ART10058>3.0.CO;2-W

[103] Eyrich D, Wiese H, Maier G, Skodacek D, Appel B, Sarhan H, et al. In vitro and in vivo cartilage engineering using a combination of chondrocyte-seeded long-term stable fibrin gels and polycaprolactone-based polyurethane scaffolds. Tissue Eng 2007 Sep;13(9):2207-2218. DOI: 10.1089/ten.2006.0358

[104] Zwingmann J, Mehlhorn AT, Sudkamp N, Stark B, Dauner M, Schmal H. Chondrogenic differentiation of human articular chondrocytes differs in biodegradable PGA/PLA scaffolds. Tissue Eng 2007 Sep;13(9):2335-2343. DOI: 10.1089/ten.2006.0393

[105] Moroni L, Hamann D, Paoluzzi L, Pieper J, de Wijn JR, van Blitterswijk CA. Regenerating articular tissue by converging technologies. PLoS ONE 2008;3(8):e3032.

[106] Fujihara Y, Asawa Y, Takato T, Hoshi K. Tissue Reactions to Engineered Cartilage Based on Poly-L-Lactic Acid Scaffolds. Tissue Eng Part A 2008 Dec 30

[107] Hidaka C, Ibarra C, Hannafin JA, Torzilli PA, Quitoriano M, Jen SS, et al. Formation of vascularized meniscal tissue by combining gene therapy with tissue engineering. Tissue Eng 2002 Feb;8(1):93-105. DOI: 10.1089/107632702753503090

[108] Marsano A, Millward-Sadler SJ, Salter DM, Adesida A, Hardingham T, Tognana E, et al. Differential cartilaginous tissue formation by human synovial membrane, fat pad, meniscus cells and articular chondrocytes. Osteoarthritis Cartilage 2007 Jan;15(1):48-58. DOI: 10.1016/j.joca.2006.06.009

[109] Peretti GM, Caruso EM, Randolph MA, Zaleske DJ. Meniscal repair using engineered tissue. J Orthop Res 2001 Mar;19(2):278-285. DOI: 10.1016/S0736-0266(00)90010-X

[110] Lee JY, Hall R, Pelinkovic D, Cassinelli E, Usas A, Gilbertson L, et al. New use of a three-dimensional pellet culture system for human intervertebral disc cells: initial characterization and potential use for tissue engineering. Spine 2001 Nov 1;26(21):2316-2322. DOI: 10.1097/00007632-200111010-00005

[111] Mizuno H, Roy AK, Vacanti CA, Kojima K, Ueda M, Bonassar LJ. Tissue-engineered composites of anulus fibrosus and nucleus pulposus for intervertebral disc replacement. Spine 2004 Jun 15;29(12):1290-1297; discussion 1297-1298. DOI: 10.1097/01.BRS.0000128264.46510.27

[112] Mizuno H, Roy AK, Zaporojan V, Vacanti CA, Ueda M, Bonassar LJ. Biomechanical and biochemical characterization of composite tissue-engineered intervertebral discs. Biomaterials 2006 Jan;27(3):362-370. DOI: 10.1016/j.biomaterials.2005.06.042

[113] Suzuki T, Bessho K, Fujimura K, Okubo Y, Segami N, Iizuka T. Regeneration of defects in the articular cartilage in rabbit temporomandibular joints by bone morphogenetic protein-2. Br J Oral Maxillofac Surg 2002 Jun;40(3):201-206.

[114] Yao X, Ma X, Zhang Z. [An experimental study on the regenerating ability of the condylar cartilage of the rabbit]. Zhonghua Kou Qiang Yi Xue Za Zhi 1998 Jul;33(4):201-203.

[115] Yao X, Ma X, Zhang Z. [The effect of prednisolone on the regeneration of condylar cartilage of the rabbit]. Zhonghua Kou Qiang Yi Xue Za Zhi 2000 Jul;35(4):277-279.

[116] Yao X, Ma X, Zhang Z. [The repairment of the condylar cartilage defect by transplantation of chondrocytes embedded in the collagen membrane]. Zhonghua Kou Qiang Yi Xue Za Zhi 2000 Mar;35(2):138-141.

[117] Yao X, Ma X, Zhang Z. Chondrocyte allografts for repair of full-thickness defects in the condylar articular cartilage of rabbits. Chin J Dent Res 2000 Nov;3(3):24-30.

[118] Ueki K, Takazakura D, Marukawa K, Shimada M, Nakagawa K, Takatsuka S, et al. The use of polylactic acid/polyglycolic acid copolymer and gelatin sponge complex containing human recombinant bone morphogenetic protein-2 following condylectomy in rabbits. J Craniomaxillofac Surg 2003 Apr;31(2):107-114.

[119] Takafuji H, Suzuki T, Okubo Y, Fujimura K, Bessho K. Regeneration of articular cartilage defects in the temporomandibular joint of rabbits by fibroblast growth factor-2: a pilot study. Int J Oral Maxillofac Surg 2007 Oct;36(10):934-937.

[120] May B, Saha S. Animal models for TMJ studies: A review of the literature. TMJournal 2000 Spring;1(1):20-27.

[121] Berg R. Contribution to the applied and topographical anatomy of the temporomandibular joint of some domestic mammals with particular reference to the partial resp. total resection of the articular disc. Folia Morphol (Praha) 1973;21(2):202-204.

[122] Strom D, Holm S, Clemensson E, Haraldson T, Carlsson GE. Gross anatomy of the mandibular joint and masticatory muscles in the domestic pig (Sus scrofa). Arch Oral Biol 1986;31(11):763-768.

[123] Springer IN, Fleiner B, Jepsen S, Acil Y. Culture of cells gained from temporomandibular joint cartilage on non-absorbable scaffolds. Biomaterials 2001 Sep;22(18):2569-2577. DOI: 10.1016/S0142-9612(01)00148-X

[124] Bermejo A, Gonzalez O, Gonzalez JM. The pig as an animal model for experimentation on the temporomandibular articular complex. Oral Surg Oral Med Oral Pathol 1993 Jan;75(1):18-23. DOI: 10.1016/0030-4220(93)90399-O

[125] Hatton MN, Swann DA. Studies on bovine temporomandibular joint synovial fluid. J Prosthet Dent 1986 Nov;56(5):635-638. DOI: 10.1016/0022-3913(86)90433-6

[126] Tanaka E, Hirose M, Yamano E, Dalla-Bona DA, Fujita R, Tanaka M, et al. Age-associated changes in viscoelastic properties of the bovine temporomandibular joint disc. Eur J Oral Sci 2006 Feb;114(1):70-73. DOI: 10.1111/j.1600-0722.2006.00265.x

[127] Tanaka E, Tanaka M, Miyawaki Y, Tanne K. Viscoelastic properties of canine temporomandibular joint disc in compressive load-relaxation. Arch Oral Biol 1999 Dec;44(12):1021-1026. DOI: 10.1016/S0003-9969(99)00097-7

[128] Shengyi T, Xu Y. Biomechanical properties and collagen fiber orientation of TMJ discs in dogs: Part 1. Gross anatomy and collagen fiber orientation of the discs. J Craniomandib Disord 1991 Winter;5(1):28-34.

[129] Bifano C, Hubbard G, Ehler W. A comparison of the form and function of the human, monkey, and goat temporomandibular joint. J Oral Maxillofac Surg 1994 Mar;52(3):272-275; discussion 276-277. DOI: 10.1016/0278-2391(94)90298-4

[130] Kurita K, Westesson PL, Eriksson L, Sternby NH. High condylar shave of the temporomandibular joint with preservation of the articular soft tissue cover: an experimental study on rabbits. Oral Surg Oral Med Oral Pathol 1990 Jan;69(1):10-14. DOI: 10.1016/0030-4220(90)90260-Y

[131] Scapino RP, Canham PB, Finlay HM, Mills DK. The behaviour of collagen fibres in stress relaxation and stress distribution in the jaw-joint disc of rabbits. Arch Oral Biol 1996 Nov;41(11):1039-1052. DOI: 10.1016/S0003-9969(96)00079-9

[132] Sakurai M, Yonemitsu I, Muramoto T, Soma K. Effects of masticatory muscle force on temporomandibular joint disc growth in rats. Arch Oral Biol 2007 Dec;52(12):1186-1193. DOI: 10.1016/j.archoralbio.2007.07.003

[133] Deschner J, Rath-Deschner B, Reimann S, Bourauel C, Gotz W, Jepsen S, et al. Regulatory effects of biophysical strain on rat TMJ discs. Ann Anat 2007;189(4):326-328.

[134] Bosanquet AG, Goss AN. The sheep as a model for temporomandibular joint surgery. Int J Oral Maxillofac Surg 1987 Oct;16(5):600-603. DOI: 10.1016/S0901-5027(87)80113-3

[135] Bosanquet AG, Ishimaru J, Goss AN. Effect of fascia repair of the temporomandibular joint disk of sheep. Oral Surg Oral Med Oral Pathol 1991 Nov;72(5):520-523. DOI: 10.1016/0030-4220(91)90486-V

[136] Detamore MS, Athanasiou KA, Mao J. A call to action for bioengineers and dental professionals: Directives for the future of TMJ bioengineering. Ann Biomed Eng 2007 Aug;35(8):1301-1311. DOI: 10.1007/s10439-007-9298-6

[137] Strom D, Holm S, Clemensson E, Haraldson T, Carlsson GE. Gross anatomy of the mandibular joint and masticatory muscles in the domestic pig (Sus scrofa). Arch Oral Biol 1986;31(11):763-768.

[138] Kuttila M, Le Bell Y, Savolainen-Niemi E, Kuttila S, Alanen P. Efficiency of occlusal appliance therapy in secondary otalgia and temporomandibular disorders. Acta Odontol Scand 2002 Aug;60(4):248-254. DOI: 10.1080/000163502760148034

[139] Forssell H, Kalso E. Application of principles of evidence-based medicine to occlusal treatment for temporomandibular disorders: are there lessons to be learned? J Orofac Pain 2004 Winter;18(1):9-22; discussion 23-32.

[140] Dionne RA. Pharmacologic approaches. In: Laskin DM, Greene CS, Hylander WL, editors. TMDs, an evidencebased approach to diagnosis and treatment. Chicago: Quintessence, 2006. p. 347-357.

[141] De Laat A, Stappaerts K, Papy S. Counseling and physical therapy as treatment for myofascial pain of the masticatory system. J Orofac Pain 2003 Winter;17(1):42-49.

[142] Nitzan DW, Price A. The use of arthrocentesis for the treatment of osteoarthritic temporomandibular joints. J Oral Maxillofac Surg 2001 Oct;59(10):1154-1159; discussion 1160. DOI: 10.1053/joms.2001.26716

[143] Holmlund A, Hellsing G, Wredmark T. Arthroscopy of the temporomandibular joint. A clinical study. Int J Oral Maxillofac Surg 1986 Dec;15(6):715-721.

[144] Mercuri LG. Surgical management of TMJ arthritis. In: Laskin DM, Greene CS, Hylander WL, editors. TMDs, an evidence-based approach to diagnosis and treatment. Chicago: Quintessence, 2006. p. 455-468.

[145] Merrill RG. Historical perspectives and comparisons of TMJ surgery for internal disk derangements and arthropathy. Cranio 1986 Jan;4(1):74-85.

[146] Feinberg SE, Larsen PE. The use of a pedicled temporalis muscle-pericranial flap for replacement of the TMJ disc: preliminary report. J Oral Maxillofac Surg 1989 Feb;47(2):142-146.

[147] Wolford LM, Cottrell DA, Henry CH. Temporomandibular joint reconstruction of the complex patient with the Techmedica custom-made total joint prosthesis. J Oral Maxillofac Surg 1994 Jan;52(1):2-10; discussion 11. DOI: 10.1016/0278-2391(94)90003-5

[148] MacIntosh RB. The use of autogenous tissues for temporomandibular joint reconstruction. J Oral Maxillofac Surg 2000 Jan;58(1):63-69. DOI: 10.1016/S0278-2391(00)80019-1

[149] Chapman MW. Chapman's orthopaedic surgery. Philadelphia: Williams & Wilkins, 2001

[150] McBride KL. Total temporomandibular joint reconstruction. In: Worthington P, Evans JR, editors. Controversies in oral and maxillofacial surgery. Philadelphia: W.B. Saunders Co., 1994. p. 381-396.

[151] Mercuri LG. Alloplastic temporomandibular reconstruction. Surg Oral Med Oral Pathol Oral Radiol Endod 1998;85:631-637.

[152] Mercuri LG. Subjective and objective outcomes in patients reconstructed with a custom-fitted alloplastic temporomandibular joint prosthesis. J Oral Maxillofac Surg 1999;57(12):1427-1430.

[153] Mercuri LG. The TMJ Concepts patient fitted total temporomandibular joint reconstruction prosthesis. Oral Maxillofac Surg Clin North Am 2000;12:73-91.

[154] Mercuri LG, Anspach WE, 3rd. Principles for the revision of total alloplastic TMJ prostheses. Int J Oral Maxillofac Surg 2003 Aug;32(4):353-359. DOI: 10.1054/ijom.2002.0447

[155] Wolford LM, Pitta MC, Reiche-Fischel O, Franco PF. TMJ Concepts/Techmedica custom-made TMJ total joint prosthesis: 5-year follow-up study. Int J Oral Maxillofac Surg 2003 Jun;32(3):268-274. DOI: 10.1054/ijom.2002.0350

[156] Mercuri LG. A rationale for total alloplastic temporomandibular joint reconstruction in the management of idiopathic/progressive condylar resorption. J Oral Maxillofac Surg 2007;65:1600-1609 erratum.

[157] Mercuri LG, Giobbie-Hurder A. Long-term outcomes after total alloplastic temporo-mandibular joint reconstruction following exposure to failed materials. J Oral Maxillofac Surg 2004 Sep;62(9):1088-1096. DOI: 10.1016/j.joms.2003.10.012

[158] Mercuri LG, Wolford LM, Sanders B, White RD, Giobbie-Hurder A. Long-term follow-up of the CAD/CAM patient fitted total temporomandibular joint reconstruction system. J Oral Maxillofac Surg 2002 Dec;60(12):1440-1448. DOI: 10.1053/joms.2002.36103

[159] Mercuri LG. A rationale for total alloplastic temporomandibular joint reconstruction in the management of idiopathic/progressive condylar resorption. J Oral Maxillofac Surg 2007 Aug;65(8):1600-1609. DOI: 10.1016/j.joms.2006.03.056

[160] Revell CM, Athanasiou KA. Success rates and immunologic responses of autogenic, allogenic, and xenogenic treatments to repair articular cartilage defects. Tissue Eng Part B Rev 2009 Mar;15(1):1-15. DOI: 10.1089/ten.teb.2008.0189

[161] Mankin HJ. The response of articular cartilage to mechanical injury. J Bone Joint Surg Am 1982 Mar;64(3):460-466.

[162] Hunziker EB. Articular cartilage repair: are the intrinsic biological constraints un-dermining this process insuperable? Osteoarthritis Cartilage 1999 Jan;7(1):15-28. DOI: 10.1053/joca.1998.0159

[163] Hangody L, Feczko P, Bartha L, Bodo G, Kish G. Mosaicplasty for the treatment of artic-ular defects of the knee and ankle. Clin Orthop Relat Res 2001 Oct(391 Suppl):S328-336. DOI: 10.1097/00003086-200110001-00030

[164] Hangody L, Kish G, Karpati Z, Szerb I, Eberhardt R. Treatment of osteochondritis dissecans of the talus: use of the mosaicplasty technique–a preliminary report. Foot Ankle Int 1997 Oct;18(10):628-634.

[165] Matsusue Y, Yamamuro T, Hama H. Arthroscopic multiple osteochondral transplantation to the chondral defect in the knee associated with anterior cruciate ligament disruption. Arthroscopy 1993;9(3):318-321.

[166] Shapiro F, Koide S, Glimcher MJ. Cell origin and differentiation in the repair of full-thickness defects of articular cartilage. J Bone Joint Surg Am 1993 Apr;75(4):532-553.

[167] Hurtig MB, Fretz PB, Doige CE, Schnurr DL. Effects of lesion size and location on equine articular cartilage repair. Can J Vet Res 1988 Jan;52(1):137-146.

[168] Convery FR, Akeson WH, Keown GH. The repair of large osteochondral defects. An experimental study in horses. Clin Orthop Relat Res 1972 Jan-Feb;82:253-262. DOI: 10.1097/00003086-197201000-00033

[169] Blevins FT, Steadman JR, Rodrigo JJ, Silliman J. Treatment of articular cartilage defects in athletes: an analysis of functional outcome and lesion appearance. Orthopedics 1998 Jul;21(7):761-767; discussion 767-768.

[170] Aston JE, Bentley G. Repair of articular surfaces by allografts of articular and growth-plate cartilage. J Bone Joint Surg Br 1986 Jan;68(1):29-35.

[171] Burks RT, Greis PE, Arnoczky SP, Scher C. The use of a single osteochondral autograft plug in the treatment of a large osteochondral lesion in the femoral condyle: an experimental study in sheep. Am J Sports Med 2006 Feb;34(2):247-255. DOI: 10.1177/0363546505279914

[172] Hangody L, Fules P. Autologous osteochondral mosaicplasty for the treatment of full-thickness defects of weight-bearing joints: ten years of experimental and clinical experience. J Bone Joint Surg Am 2003;85-A Suppl 2:25-32.

[173] Marcacci M, Kon E, Zaffagnini S, Visani A. Use of autologous grafts for reconstruction of osteochondral defects of the knee. Orthopedics 1999 Jun;22(6):595-600.

[174] Meyers MH, Akeson W, Convery FR. Resurfacing of the knee with fresh osteochondral allograft. J Bone Joint Surg Am 1989 Jun;71(5):704-713.

[175] von Rechenberg B, Akens MK, Nadler D, Bittmann P, Zlinszky K, Kutter A, et al. Changes in subchondral bone in cartilage resurfacing–an experimental study in sheep using different types of osteochondral grafts. Osteoarthritis Cartilage 2003 Apr;11(4):265-277. DOI: 10.1016/S1063-4584(03)00006-2

[176] Brittberg M, Peterson L, Sjogren-Jansson E, Tallheden T, Lindahl A. Articular cartilage engineering with autologous chondrocyte transplantation. A review of recent developments. J Bone Joint Surg Am 2003;85-A Suppl 3:109-115.

[177] Romaniuk A, Malejczyk J, Kubicka U, Hyc A, Olszewski WL, Moskalewski S. Rejection of cartilage formed by transplanted allogeneic chondrocytes: evaluation with monoclonal antibodies. Transpl Immunol 1995 Sep;3(3):251-257. DOI: 10.1016/0966-3274(95)80032-8

[178] Jiang CC, Chiang H, Liao CJ, Lin YJ, Kuo TF, Shieh CS, et al. Repair of porcine articular cartilage defect with a biphasic osteochondral composite. J Orthop Res 2007 Oct;25(10):1277-1290. DOI: 10.1002/jor.20442

[179] Fragonas E, Valente M, Pozzi-Mucelli M, Toffanin R, Rizzo R, Silvestri F, et al. Articular cartilage repair in rabbits by using suspensions of allogenic chondrocytes in alginate. Biomaterials 2000 Apr;21(8):795-801. DOI: 10.1016/S0142-9612(99)00241-0

[180] Fuentes-Boquete I, Lopez-Armada MJ, Maneiro E, Fernandez-Sueiro JL, Carames B, Galdo F, et al. Pig chondrocyte xenoimplants for human chondral defect

repair: an in vitro model. Wound Repair Regen 2004 Jul-Aug;12(4):444-452. DOI: 10.1111/j.1067-1927.2004.012412.x

[181] Hale DA. Basic transplantation immunology. Surg Clin North Am 2006 Oct;86(5):1103-1125, v. DOI: 10.1016/j.suc.2006.06.015

[182] Pietra BA. Transplantation immunology 2003: simplified approach. Pediatr Clin North Am 2003 Dec;50(6):1233-1259. DOI: 10.1016/S0031-3955(03)00119-6

[183] Trivedi HL. Immunobiology of rejection and adaptation. Transplant Proc 2007 Apr;39(3):647-652. DOI: 10.1016/j.transproceed.2007.01.047

[184] Goldsby RA, Kindt TJ, Osborne BA, Kuby J. Immunology. 5th ed. New York: W. H. Freeman and Company, 2003

[185] Bolano L, Kopta JA. The immunology of bone and cartilage transplantation. Orthopedics 1991 Sep;14(9):987-996.

[186] Moskalewski S, Hyc A, Osiecka-Iwan A. Immune response by host after allogeneic chondrocyte transplant to the cartilage. Microsc Res Tech 2002 Jul 1;58(1):3-13. DOI: 10.1002/jemt.10110

[187] Lance EM. Immunological reactivity towards chondrocytes in rat and man: relevance to autoimmune arthritis. Immunol Lett 1989 Apr;21(1):63-73. DOI: 10.1016/0165-2478(89)90013-8

[188] Malejczyk J. Natural anti-chondrocyte cytotoxicity of normal human peripheral blood mononuclear cells. Clin Immunol Immunopathol 1989 Jan;50(1 Pt 1):42-52. DOI: 10.1016/0090-1229(89)90220-1

[189] Malejczyk J, Kaminski MJ, Malejczyk M, Majewski S. Natural cell-mediated cytotoxic activity against isolated chondrocytes in the mouse. Clin Exp Immunol 1985 Jan;59(1):110-116.

[190] Yamaga KM, Kimura LH, Plymyer MR, Glant TT, Lance EM. Differentiation antigens of human articular chondrocytes and their tissue distribution as assessed by monoclonal antibodies. J Autoimmun 1994 Apr;7(2):203-217. DOI: 10.1006/jaut.1994.1016

[191] Bujia J, Alsalameh S, Naumann A, Wilmes E, Sittinger M, Burmester GR. Humoral immune response against minor collagens type IX and XI in patients with cartilage graft resorption after reconstructive surgery. Ann Rheum Dis 1994 Apr;53(4):229-234. DOI: 10.1136/ard.53.4.229

[192] Dayer E, Mathai L, Glant TT, Mikecz K, Poole AR. Cartilage proteoglycan-induced arthritis in BALB/c mice. Antibodies that recognize human and mouse cartilage proteoglycan and can cause depletion of cartilage proteoglycan with little or no synovitis. Arthritis Rheum 1990 Sep;33(9):1394-1405. DOI: 10.1002/art.1780330912

[193] Glant TT, Buzas EI, Finnegan A, Negroiu G, Cs-Szabo G, Mikecz K. Critical roles of glycosaminoglycan side chains of cartilage proteoglycan (aggrecan) in antigen recognition and presentation. J Immunol 1998 Apr 15;160(8):3812-3819.

[194] Takagi T, Jasin HE. Interactions between anticollagen antibodies and chondrocytes. Arthritis Rheum 1992 Feb;35(2):224-230. DOI: 10.1002/art.1780350217

[195] Yablon IG, Cooperband S, Covall D. Matrix antigens in allografts. The humoral response. Clin Orthop Relat Res 1982 Aug(168):243-251.

[196] Dolwick MF. Diagnosis and etiology. In: Helms CA, Katzberg RW, Dolwick MF, editors. Internal Derangements of the Temporomandibular Joint. San Francisco, CA: Radiology Research and Education Foundation, 1983. p. 31-42.

[197] Warren MP, Fried JL. Temporomandibular disorders and hormones in women. Cells Tissues Organs 2001;169(3):187-192.

[198] Ware WH. Clinical presentation. In: Helms CA, Katzberg RW, Dolwick MF, editors. Internal Derangements of the Temporomandibular Joint. San Francisco, CA: Radiology Research and Education Foundation, 1983. p. 15-30.

[199] Nilsson IM, List T, Drangsholt M. Prevalence of temporomandibular pain and subsequent dental treatment in Swedish adolescents. J Orofac Pain 2005 Spring;19(2):144-150.

[200] Isong U, Gansky SA, Plesh O. Temporomandibular joint and muscle disorder-type pain in U.S. adults: the National Health Interview Survey. J Orofac Pain 2008 Fall;22(4):317-322.

[201] Piette E. Anatomy of the human temporomandibular joint. An updated comprehensive review. Acta Stomatol Belg 1993;90(2):103-127.

[202] Jagger RG, Bates JF, Kopp S. Temporomandibular Joint Dysfunction: Essentials. Oxford: Butterworth-Heinemann Ltd., 1994

[203] Ogus HD, Toller PA. Common Disorders of the Temporomandibular Joint. 2nd edition ed. Bristol: John Wright & Sons Ltd, 1986

[204] Werner JA, Tillmann B, Schleicher A. Functional anatomy of the temporomandibular joint. A morphologic study on human autopsy material. Anat Embryol 1991;183(1):89-95.

[205] Haskin CL, Milam SB, Cameron IL. Pathogenesis of degenerative joint disease in the human temporomandibular joint. Crit Rev Oral Biol Med 1995;6(3):248-277.

[206] Bragdon EE, Light KC, Costello NL, Sigurdsson A, Bunting S, Bhalang K, et al. Group differences in pain modulation: pain-free women compared to pain-free men and to women with TMD. Pain 2002 Apr;96(3):227-237. DOI: 10.1016/S0304-3959(01)00451-1

[207] Bereiter DA. Sex differences in brainstem neural activation after injury to the TMJ region. Cells Tissues Organs 2001;169(3):226-237.

[208] Thut PD, Hermanstyne TO, Flake NM, Gold MS. An operant conditioning model to assess changes in feeding behavior associated with temporomandibular joint inflammation in the rat. J Orofac Pain 2007 Winter;21(1):7-18.

[209] Harriott AM, Dessem D, Gold MS. Inflammation increases the excitability of masseter muscle afferents. Neuroscience 2006 Aug 11;141(1):433-442. DOI: 10.1016/j.neuroscience.2006.03.049

[210] Flake NM, Hermanstyne TO, Gold MS. Testosterone and estrogen have opposing actions on inflammation-induced plasma extravasation in the rat temporomandibular joint. Am J Physiol Regul Integr Comp Physiol 2006 Aug;291(2):R343-348.

[211] Flake NM, Gold MS. Inflammation alters sodium currents and excitability of temporomandibular joint afferents. Neurosci Lett 2005 Aug 26;384(3):294-299. DOI: 10.1016/j.neulet.2005.04.091

[212] Flake NM, Bonebreak DB, Gold MS. Estrogen and inflammation increase the excitability of rat temporomandibular joint afferent neurons. J Neurophysiol 2005 Mar;93(3):1585-1597. DOI: 10.1152/jn.00269.2004

[213] Detamore MS, Athanasiou KA. Motivation, characterization, and strategy for tissue engineering the temporomandibular joint disc. Tissue Eng 2003 Dec;9(6):1065-1087. DOI: 10.1089/10763270360727991

[214] Gage JP, Shaw RM, Moloney FB. Collagen type in dysfunctional temporomandibular joint disks. J Prosthet Dent 1995;74(5):517-520.

[215] Nakano T, Scott PG. Proteoglycans of the articular disc of the bovine temporomandibular joint. I. High molecular weight chondroitin sulphate proteoglycan. Matrix 1989;9(4):277-283.

[216] Almarza AJ, Bean AC, Baggett LS, Athanasiou KA. Biochemical analysis of the porcine temporomandibular joint disc. Br J Oral Maxillofac Surg 2006 Apr;44(2):124-128. DOI: 10.1016/j.bjoms.2005.05.002

[217] Berkovitz BK, Robertshaw H. Ultrastructural quantification of collagen in the articular disc of the temporomandibular joint of the rabbit. Arch Oral Biol 1993 Jan;38(1):91-95. DOI: 10.1016/0003-9969(93)90161-E

[218] Mills DK, Fiandaca DJ, Scapino RP. Morphologic, microscopic, and immunohistochemical investigations into the function of the primate TMJ disc. J Orofac Pain 1994;8(2):136-154.

[219] Landesberg R, Takeuchi E, Puzas JE. Cellular, biochemical and molecular characterization of the bovine temporomandibular joint disc. Arch Oral Biol 1996;41(8-9):761-767.

[220] Detamore MS, Orfanos JG, Almarza AJ, French MM, Wong ME, Athanasiou KA. Quantitative analysis and comparative regional investigation of the extracellular matrix of the porcine temporomandibular joint disc. Matrix Biol 2005 Feb;24(1):45-57.

[221] Hirschmann PN, Shuttleworth CA. The collagen composition of the mandibular joint of the foetal calf. Arch Oral Biol 1976;21(12):771-773.

[222] Carvalho RS, Yen EH, Suga DM. The effect of growth on collagen and glycosaminoglycans in the articular disc of the rat temporomandibular joint. Arch Oral Biol 1993;38(6):457-466.

[223] Ali AM, Sharawy MM. An immunohistochemical study of collagen types III, VI and IX in rabbit craniomandibular joint tissues following surgical induction of anterior disk displacement. J Oral Pathol Med 1996;25(2):78-85.

[224] Taguchi N, Nakata S, Oka T. Three-dimensional observation of the temporomandibular joint disk in the rhesus monkey. J Oral Surg 1980;38(1):11-15.

[225] Minarelli AM, Del Santo Junior M, Liberti EA. The structure of the human temporomandibular joint disc: a scanning electron microscopy study. J Orofac Pain 1997;11(2):95-100.

[226] Scapino RP, Obrez A, Greising D. Organization and function of the collagen fiber system in the human temporomandibular joint disk and its attachments. Cells Tissues Organs 2006;182(3-4):201-225.

[227] Nagy NB, Daniel JC. Distribution of elastic fibres in the developing rabbit craniomandibular joint. Arch Oral Biol 1991;36(1):15-23.

[228] de Bont LG, Liem RS, Havinga P, Boering G. Fibrous component of the temporomandibular joint disk. Cranio 1985 Sep-Dec;3(4):368-373.

[229] Teng S, Xu Y. Biomechanical properties and collagen fiber orientation of TMJ discs in dogs: Part 1. Gross anatomy and collagen fiber orientation of the discs. J Craniomandib Disord 1991 Winter;5(1):28-34.

[230] Berkovitz BK. Crimping of collagen in the intra-articular disc of the temporomandibular joint: a comparative study. J Oral Rehabil 2000;27(7):608-613.

[231] Berkovitz BK. Collagen crimping in the intra-articular disc and articular surfaces of the human temporomandibular joint. Arch Oral Biol 2000;45(9):749-756.

[232] Keith DA. Elastin in the bovine mandibular joint. Arch Oral Biol 1979;24(3):211-215.

[233] Griffin CJ, Sharpe CJ. Distribution of elastic tissue in the human temporomandibular meniscus especially in respect to "comparison" areas. Aust Dent J 1962 February;7:72-78. DOI: 10.1111/j.1834-7819.1962.tb05713.x

[234] O'Dell NL, Sharawy M, Pennington CB, Marlow RK. Distribution of putative elastic fibers in rabbit temporomandibular joint tissues. Acta Anat 1989;135(3):239-244.

[235] O'Dell NL, Starcher BC, Wilson JT, Pennington CB, Jones GA. Morphological and biochemical evidence for elastic fibres in the Syrian hamster temporomandibular joint disc. Arch Oral Biol 1990;35(10):807-811.

[236] Christensen LV. Elastic tissue in the temporomandibular disc of miniature swine. J Oral Rehabil 1975;2:373-377.

[237] Gross A, Bumann A, Hoffmeister B. Elastic fibers in the human temporo-mandibular joint disc. Int J Oral Maxillofac Surg 1999;28(6):464-468.

[238] Scott JE, Orford CR, Hughes EW. Proteoglycan-collagen arrangements in developing rat tail tendon. An electron microscopical and biochemical investigation. Biochem J 1981 Jun 1;195(3):573-581.

[239] Stander M, Naumann U, Wick W, Weller M. Transforming growth factor-beta and p-21: multiple molecular targets of decorin-mediated suppression of neoplastic growth. Cell Tissue Res 1999 May;296(2):221-227. DOI: 10.1007/s004410051283

[240] Axelsson S, Holmlund A, Hjerpe A. Glycosaminoglycans in normal and osteoarthrotic human temporomandibular joint disks. Acta Odontol Scand 1992;50(2):113-119.

[241] Nakano T, Scott PG. A quantitative chemical study of glycosaminoglycans in the articular disc of the bovine temporomandibular joint. Arch Oral Biol 1989;34(9):749-757.

[242] Almarza AJ, Athanasiou KA. Design characteristics for the tissue engineering of cartilaginous tissues. Ann Biomed Eng 2004 Jan;32(1):2-17. DOI: 10.1023/B:ABME.0000007786.37957.65

[243] Kopp S. Topographical distribution of sulphated glycosaminoglycans in human temporomandibular joint disks. A histochemical study of an autopsy material. J Oral Pathol 1976;5(5):265-276.

[244] Nakano T, Scott PG. Changes in the chemical composition of the bovine temporomandibular joint disc with age. Arch Oral Biol 1996;41(8-9):845-853.

[245] Axelsson S. Human and experimental osteoarthrosis of the temporomandibular joint. Morphological and biochemical studies. Swed Dent J Suppl 1993;92:1-45.

[246] Krusius T, Ruoslahti E. Primary structure of an extracellular matrix proteoglycan core protein deduced from cloned cDNA. Proc Natl Acad Sci U S A 1986 Oct;83(20):7683-7687. DOI: 10.1073/pnas.83.20.7683

[247] Corsi A, Xu T, Chen XD, Boyde A, Liang J, Mankani M, et al. Phenotypic effects of biglycan deficiency are linked to collagen fibril abnormalities, are synergized by decorin deficiency, and mimic Ehlers-Danlos-like changes in bone and other connective tissues. J Bone Miner Res 2002 Jul;17(7):1180-1189. DOI: 10.1359/jbmr.2002.17.7.1180

[248] Reed CC, Iozzo RV. The role of decorin in collagen fibrillogenesis and skin homeostasis. Glycoconj J 2002 May-Jun;19(4-5):249-255.

[249] Scott PG, Nakano T, Dodd CM. Small proteoglycans from different regions of the fibrocartilaginous temporomandibular joint disc. Biochim Biophys Acta 1995;1244(1):121-128.

[250] Teng S, Xu Y, Cheng M, Li Y. Biomechanical properties and collagen fiber orientation of TMJ discs in dogs: Part 2. Tensile mechanical properties of the discs. J Craniomandib Disord 1991;5(2):107-114.

[251] Tanaka E, Shibaguchi T, Tanaka M, Tanne K. Viscoelastic properties of the human temporomandibular joint disc in patients with internal derangement. J Oral Maxillofac Surg 2000;58(9):997-1002.

[252] Beek M, Aarnts MP, Koolstra JH, Feilzer AJ, van Eijden TM. Dynamic properties of the human temporomandibular joint disc. J Dent Res 2001 Mar;80(3):876-880. DOI: 10.1177/00220345010800030601

[253] Venn M, Maroudas A. Chemical composition and swelling of normal and osteoarthrotic femoral head cartilage. I. Chemical composition. Ann Rheum Dis 1977 Apr;36(2):121-129. DOI: 10.1136/ard.36.2.121

[254] Allen KD, Athanasiou KA. Viscoelastic characterization of the porcine temporomandibular joint disc under unconfined compression. J Biomech 2006;39(2):312-322.

[255] Singh M, Detamore MS. Stress relaxation behavior of mandibular condylar cartilage under high-strain compression. J Biomech Eng 2009;Epub

[256] Allen KD, Athanasiou KA. A surface-regional and freeze-thaw characterization of the porcine temporomandibular joint disc. Ann Biomed Eng 2005 Jul;33(7):951-962. DOI: 10.1007/s10439-005-3872-6

[257] Yanaki T, Yamaguchi T. Temporary network formation of hyaluronate under a physiological condition. 1. Molecular-weight dependence. Biopolymers 1990;30(3-4):415-425.

[258] Nickel JC, McLachlan KR. In vitro measurement of the frictional properties of the temporo-mandibular joint disc. Arch Oral Biol 1994;39(4):323-331.

[259] Tanaka E, Kawai N, Tanaka M, Todoh M, van Eijden T, Hanaoka K, et al. The frictional coefficient of the temporomandibular joint and its dependency on the magnitude and duration of joint loading. J Dent Res 2004 May;83(5):404-407. DOI: 10.1177/154405910408300510

[260] Nickel JC, Iwasaki LR, Beatty MW, Moss MA, Marx DB. Static and dynamic loading effects on temporomandibular joint disc tractional forces. J Dent Res 2006 Sep;85(9):809-813.

[261] Wilson W, van Burken C, van Donkelaar C, Buma P, van Rietbergen B, Huiskes R. Causes of mechanically induced collagen damage in articular cartilage. J Orthop Res 2006 Feb;24(2):220-228. DOI: 10.1002/jor.20027

[262] Zhu W, Chern KY, Mow VC. Anisotropic viscoelastic shear properties of bovine meniscus. Clin Orthop Relat Res 1994 Sep(306):34-45.

[263] Zhu W, Mow VC, Koob TJ, Eyre DR. Viscoelastic shear properties of articular carti-lage and the effects of glycosidase treatments. J Orthop Res 1993 Nov;11(6):771-781. DOI: 10.1002/jor.1100110602

[264] Tanaka E, Tanne K, Sakuda M. A three-dimensional finite element model of the mandible including the TMJ and its application to stress analysis in the TMJ during clenching. Med Eng Phys 1994;16(4):316-322.

[265] Lai WF, Bowley J, Burch JG. Evaluation of shear stress of the human temporomandibular joint disc. J Orofac Pain 1998;12(2):153-159.

[266] Tanaka E, Kawai N, Hanaoka K, Van Eijden T, Sasaki A, Aoyama J, et al. Shear properties of the temporomandibular joint disc in relation to compressive and shear strain. J Dent Res 2004 Jun;83(6):476-479. DOI: 10.1177/154405910408300608

[267] Spirt AA, Mak AF, Wassell RP. Nonlinear viscoelastic properties of articular cartilage in shear. J Orthop Res 1989;7(1):43-49.

[268] Detamore MS, Hegde JN, Wagle RR, Almarza AJ, Montufar-Solis D, Duke PJ, et al. Cell type and distribution in the porcine temporomandibular joint disc. J Oral Maxillofac Surg 2006 Feb;64(2):243-248. DOI: 10.1016/j.joms.2005.10.009

[269] Milam SB, Klebe RJ, Triplett RG, Herbert D. Characterization of the extracellular matrix of the primate temporomandibular joint. J Oral Maxillofac Surg 1991;49(4):381-391.

[270] Berkovitz BK, Pacy J. Age changes in the cells of the intra-articular disc of the temporo-mandibular joints of rats and marmosets. Arch Oral Biol 2000;45(11):987-995.

[271] Berkovitz BK, Pacy J. Ultrastructure of the human intra-articular disc of the temporomandibular joint. Eur J Orthod 2002 Apr;24(2):151-158. DOI: 10.1093/ejo/24.2.151

[272] Mills DK, Daniel JC, Scapino R. Histological features and in-vitro proteoglycan synthesis in the rabbit craniomandibular joint disc. Arch Oral Biol 1988;33(3):195-202.

[273] Kapila S, Lee C, Richards DW. Characterization and identification of proteinases and proteinase inhibitors synthesized by temporomandibular joint disc cells. J Dent Res 1995;74(6):1328-1336.

[274] Currey JD. Changes in the impact energy absorption of bone with age. J Biomech 1979;12(6):459-469.

[275] Vogel HG. Influence of maturation and aging on mechanical and biochemical properties of connective tissue in rats. Mech Ageing Dev 1980 Nov-Dec;14(3-4):283-292. DOI: 10.1016/0047-6374(80)90002-0

[276] Tanaka E, Tanaka M, Hattori Y, Aoyama J, Watanabe M, Sasaki A, et al. Biomechanical behaviour of bovine temporomandibular articular discs with age. Arch Oral Biol 2001 Nov;46(11):997-1003. DOI: 10.1016/S0003-9969(01)00072-3

[277] Carvalho RS, Yen EH, Suga DM. Glycosaminoglycan synthesis in the rat articular disk in response to mechanical stress. Am J Orthod Dentofacial Orthop 1995;107(4):401-410.

[278] Palmoski MJ, Brandt KD. Effects of static and cyclic compressive loading on articular cartilage plugs in vitro. Arthritis Rheum 1984 Jun;27(6):675-681. DOI: 10.1002/art.1780270611

[279] Parkkinen JJ, Lammi MJ, Helminen HJ, Tammi M. Local stimulation of proteoglycan synthesis in articular cartilage explants by dynamic compression in vitro. J Orthop Res 1992 Sep;10(5):610-620. DOI: 10.1002/jor.1100100503

[280] Kiviranta I, Tammi M, Jurvelin J, Saamanen AM, Helminen HJ. Moderate running exercise augments glycosaminoglycans and thickness of articular cartilage in the knee joint of young beagle dogs. J Orthop Res 1988;6(2):188-195.

[281] Ahn HJ, Paik SK, Choi JK, Kim HJ, Ahn DK, Cho YS, et al. Age-related changes in the microarchitecture of collagen fibrils in the articular disc of the rat temporomandibular joint. Arch Histol Cytol 2007 Oct;70(3):175-181. DOI: 10.1679/aohc.70.175

[282] Parry DA. The molecular and fibrillar structure of collagen and its relationship to the mechanical properties of connective tissue. Biophys Chem 1988 Feb;29(1-2):195-209. DOI: 10.1016/0301-4622(88)87039-X

[283] Diamant J, Keller A, Baer E, Litt M, Arridge RG. Collagen; ultrastructure and its relation to mechanical properties as a function of ageing. Proc R Soc Lond B Biol Sci 1972 Mar 14;180(60):293-315. DOI: 10.1098/rspb.1972.0019

[284] Carlsson GE, Oberg T, Bergman F, Fajers CM. Morphological changes in the mandibular joint disk in temporomandibular joint pain dysfunction syndrome. Acta Odontol Scand 1967 Aug;25(2):163-181. DOI: 10.3109/00016356709028745

[285] Piacentini C, Marchetti C, Callegari A, Setti M, Bernasconi G, Baciliero U, et al. Endoarticular loose bodies and calcifications of the disk of the temporomandibular joint: morphological features and chemical composition. Scanning Microsc 1995 Sep;9(3):789-795; discussion 796.

[286] Hansson T, Oberg T, Carlsson GE, Kopp S. Thickness of the soft tissue layers and the articular disk in the temporomandibular joint. Acta Odontol Scand 1977 May;35(2):77-83. DOI: 10.3109/00016357709055993

[287] Hansson T, Nordstrom B. Thickness of the soft tissue layers and articular disk in temporomandibular joints with deviations in form. Acta Odontol Scand 1977;35(6):281-

[288] Bibb CA, Pullinger AG, Baldioceda F. Serial variation in histological character of articular soft tissue in young human adult temporomandibular joint condyles. Arch Oral Biol 1993 Apr;38(4):343-352. DOI: 10.1016/0003-9969(93)90142-9

[289] Pullinger AG, Baldioceda F, Bibb CA. Relationship of TMJ articular soft tissue to underlying bone in young adult condyles. J Dent Res 1990 Aug;69(8):1512-1518.

[290] Bosshardt-Luehrs CP, Luder HU. Cartilage matrix production and chondrocyte enlargement as contributors to mandibular condylar growth in monkeys (Macaca fascicularis). Am J Orthod Dentofacial Orthop 1991 Oct;100(4):362-369. DOI: 10.1016/0889-5406(91)70075-8

[291] Lu XL, Mow VC, Guo XE. Proteoglycans and mechanical behavior of condylar cartilage. J Dent Res 2009 Mar;88(3):244-248.

[292] Luder HU, Schroeder HE. Light and electron microscopic morphology of the temporomandibular joint in growing and mature crab-eating monkeys (Macaca fascicularis): the condylar articular layer. Anat Embryol (Berl) 1990;181(5):499-511.

[293] Mizoguchi I, Takahashi I, Nakamura M, Sasano Y, Sato S, Kagayama M, et al. An immunohistochemical study of regional differences in the distribution of type I and type II collagens in rat mandibular condylar cartilage. Arch Oral Biol 1996 Aug-Sep;41(8-9):863-869. DOI: 10.1016/S0003-9969(96)00021-0

[294] Silbermann M, Frommer J. The nature of endochondral ossification in the mandibular condyle of the mouse. Anat Rec 1972 Apr;172(4):659-667. DOI: 10.1002/ar.1091720406

[295] Zhao Z, Rabie AB, Urban H, Shen G. [Image analysis of condylar cartilaginous adaptation to mandibular protrusion in rats]. Hua Xi Kou Qiang Yi Xue Za Zhi 1999 May;17(2):155-158.

[296] Durkin JF, Heeley JD, Irving JT. The cartilage of the mandibular condyle. Oral Sci Rev 1973;2:29-99.

[297] Singh M, Detamore MS. Biomechanical properties of the mandibular condylar cartilage and their relevance to the TMJ disc. J Biomech 2009;Accepted

[298] Wang L, Detamore MS. Tissue engineering the mandibular condyle. Tissue Eng 2007 Aug;13(8):1955-1971. DOI: 10.1089/ten.2006.0152

[299] Burrows AM, Smith TD. Histomorphology of the mandibular condylar cartilage in greater galagos (Otolemur spp.). Am J Primatol 2007 Jan;69(1):36-45. DOI: 10.1002/ajp.20325

[300] Shibata S, Baba O, Ohsako M, Suzuki S, Yamashita Y, Ichijo T. Ultrastructural observation on matrix fibers in the condylar cartilage of the adult rat mandible. Bull Tokyo Med Dent Univ 1991 Dec;38(4):53-61.

[301] Delatte M, Von den Hoff JW, van Rheden RE, Kuijpers-Jagtman AM. Primary and secondary cartilages of the neonatal rat: the femoral head and the mandibular condyle. Eur J Oral Sci 2004 Apr;112(2):156-162. DOI: 10.1111/j.0909-8836.2004.00108.x

[302] Wang L, Lazebnik M, Detamore MS. Hyaline cartilage cells outperform mandibular condylar cartilage cells in a TMJ fibrocartilage tissue engineering application. Osteoarthritis Cartilage 2009 Mar;17(3):346-353. DOI: 10.1016/j.joca.2008.07.004

[303] Teramoto M, Kaneko S, Shibata S, Yanagishita M, Soma K. Effect of compressive forces on extracellular matrix in rat mandibular condylar cartilage. J Bone Miner Metab 2003;21(5):276-286.

[304] Pietila K, Kantomaa T, Pirttiniemi P, Poikela A. Comparison of amounts and properties of collagen and proteoglycans in condylar, costal and nasal cartilages. Cells Tissues Organs 1999;164(1):30-36.

[305] de Bont LG, Boering G, Havinga P, Liem RS. Spatial arrangement of collagen fibrils in the articular cartilage of the mandibular condyle: a light microscopic and scanning electron microscopic study. J Oral Maxillofac Surg 1984 May;42(5):306-313. DOI: 10.1016/0278-2391(84)90110-1

[306] Klinge RF. The structure of the mandibular condyle in the monkey (Macaca mulatta). Micron 1996 Oct;27(5):381-387. DOI: 10.1016/S0968-4328(96)00038-8

[307] Mizuno I, Saburi N, Taguchi N, Kaneda T, Hoshino T. The fine structure of the fibrous zone of articular cartilage in the rat mandibular condyle. Shika Kiso Igakkai Zasshi 1990 Feb;32(1):69-79.

[308] Appleton J. The ultrastructure of the articular tissue of the mandibular condyle in the rat. Arch Oral Biol 1975 Dec;20(12):823-826. DOI: 10.1016/0003-9969(75)90060-6

[309] Poikela A, Kantomaa T, Pirttiniemi P, Tuukkanen J, Pietila K. Unilateral masticatory function changes the proteoglycan content of mandibular condylar cartilage in rabbit. Cells Tissues Organs 2000;167(1):49-57.

[310] Roth S, Muller K, Fischer DC, Dannhauer KH. Specific properties of the extracellular chondroitin sulphate proteoglycans in the mandibular condylar growth centre in pigs. Arch Oral Biol 1997;42(1):63-76.

[311] Mao JJ, Rahemtulla F, Scott PG. Proteoglycan expression in the rat temporomandibular joint in response to unilateral bite raise. J Dent Res 1998;77(7):1520-1528.

[312] Kantomaa T, Pirttiniemi P. Changes in proteoglycan and collagen content in the mandibular condylar cartilage of the rabbit caused by an altered relationship between the condyle and glenoid fossa. Eur J Orthod 1998 Aug;20(4):435-441. DOI: 10.1093/ejo/20.4.435

[313] Kantomaa T, Pirttiniemi P, Tuominen M, Poikela A. Glycosaminoglycan synthesis in the mandibular condyle during growth adaptation. Acta Anat (Basel) 1994;151(2):88-96.

[314] Del Santo M, Jr., Marches F, Ng M, Hinton RJ. Age-associated changes in decorin in rat mandibular condylar cartilage. Arch Oral Biol 2000 Jun;45(6):485-493. DOI: 10.1016/S0003-9969(00)00013-3

[315] Nomura T, Gold E, Powers MP, Shingaki S, Katz JL. Micromechanics/structure relationships in the human mandible. Dent Mater 2003 May;19(3):167-173. DOI: 10.1016/S0109-5641(02)00026-X

[316] Teng S, Herring SW. A stereological study of trabecular architecture in the mandibular condyle of the pig. Arch Oral Biol 1995 Apr;40(4):299-310. DOI: 10.1016/0003-9969(94)00173-9

[317] Singh M, Detamore MS. Biomechanical properties of the mandibular condylar cartilage and their relevance to the TMJ disc. J Biomech 2009 Mar 11;42(4):405-417. DOI: 10.1016/j.jbiomech.2008.12.012

[318] Kang H, Bao G, Dong Y, Yi X, Chao Y, Chen M. [Tensile mechanics of mandibular condylar cartilage]. Hua Xi Kou Qiang Yi Xue Za Zhi 2000 Apr;18(2):85-87.

[319] Tanaka E, Hirose M, Koolstra JH, van Eijden TM, Iwabuchi Y, Fujita R, et al. Modeling of the effect of friction in the temporomandibular joint on displacement of its disc during prolonged clenching. J Oral Maxillofac Surg 2008 Mar;66(3):462-468. DOI: 10.1016/j.joms.2007.06.640

[320] Kuboki T, Shinoda M, Orsini MG, Yamashita A. Viscoelastic properties of the pig temporo-mandibular joint articular soft tissues of the condyle and disc. J Dent Res 1997;76(11):1760-1769.

[321] Patel RV, Mao JJ. Microstructural and elastic properties of the extracellular matrices of the superficial zone of neonatal articular cartilage by atomic force microscopy. Front Biosci 2003 Jan 1;8:a18-25. DOI: 10.2741/932

[322] Hu K, Radhakrishnan P, Patel RV, Mao JJ. Regional structural and viscoelastic properties of fibrocartilage upon dynamic nanoindentation of the articular condyle. J Struct Biol 2001 Oct;136(1):46-52. DOI: 10.1006/jsbi.2001.4417

[323] Copray JC, Liem RS. Ultrastructural changes associated with weaning in the mandibular condyle of the rat. Acta Anat (Basel) 1989;134(1):35-47.

[324] Silva DG, Hart JA. Ultrastructural observations on the mandibular condyle of the guinea pig. J Ultrastruct Res 1967 Oct 10;20(3):227-243. DOI: 10.1016/S0022-5320(67)90284-5

[325] Blackwood HJ. Growth of the mandibular condyle of the rat studied with tritiated thymidine. Arch Oral Biol 1966 May;11(5):493-500. DOI: 10.1016/0003-9969(66)90155-5

[326] Bibb CA, Pullinger AG, Baldioceda F. The relationship of undifferentiated mesenchymal cells to TMJ articular tissue thickness. J Dent Res 1992 Nov;71(11):1816-1821.

[327] Detamore MS, Athanasiou KA. Evaluation of three growth factors for TMJ disc tissue engineering. Ann Biomed Eng 2005 Mar;33(3):383-390. DOI: 10.1007/s10439-005-1741-y

[328] Allen KD, Athanasiou KA. Growth factor effects on passaged TMJ disk cells in monolayer and pellet cultures. Orthod Craniofac Res 2006 Aug;9(3):143-152. DOI: 10.1111/j.1601-6343.2006.00370.x

[329] Johns DE, Athanasiou KA. Improving culture conditions for temporomandibular joint disc tissue engineering. Cells Tissues Organs 2007;185(4):246-257.

[330] Allen KD, Erickson K, Athanasiou KA. The effects of protein-coated surfaces on passaged porcine TMJ disc cells. Arch Oral Biol 2008 Jan;53(1):53-59. DOI: 10.1016/j.archoralbio.2007.07.004

[331] Allen KD, Athanasiou KA. Scaffold and growth factor selection in temporomandibular joint disc engineering. J Dent Res 2008 Feb;87(2):180-185. DOI: 10.1177/154405910808700205

[332] Johns DE, Athanasiou KA. Growth factor effects on costal chondrocytes for tissue engineering fibrocartilage. Cell Tissue Res 2008 Sep;333(3):439-447. DOI: 10.1007/s00441-008-0652-2

[333] Anderson DE, Athanasiou KA. Passaged goat costal chondrocytes provide a feasible cell source for temporomandibular joint tissue engineering. Ann Biomed Eng 2008 Dec;36(12):1992-2001. DOI: 10.1007/s10439-008-9572-2

[334] Anderson DE, Athanasiou KA. A comparison of primary and passaged chondrocytes for use in engineering the temporomandibular joint. Arch Oral Biol 2009 Feb;54(2):138-145. DOI: 10.1016/j.archoralbio.2008.09.018

[335] Wang L, Detamore MS. Effects of growth factors and glucosamine on porcine mandibular condylar cartilage cells and hyaline cartilage cells for tissue engineering applications. Arch Oral Biol 2009 Jan;54(1):1-5. DOI: 10.1016/j.archoralbio.2008.06.002

[336] Klompmaker J, Jansen HW, Veth RP, Nielsen HK, de Groot JH, Pennings AJ. Porous implants for knee joint meniscus reconstruction: a preliminary study on the role of pore sizes in ingrowth and differentiation of fibrocartilage. Clin Mater 1993;14(1):1-11.

[337] Aufderheide AC, Athanasiou KA. Comparison of scaffolds and culture conditions for tissue engineering of the knee meniscus. Tissue Eng 2005 Jul-Aug;11(7-8):1095-1104. DOI: 10.1089/ten.2005.11.1095

[338] Kang SW, Son SM, Lee JS, Lee ES, Lee KY, Park SG, et al. Regeneration of whole meniscus using meniscal cells and polymer scaffolds in a rabbit total meniscectomy model. J Biomed Mater Res A 2006 Sep 1;78(3):659-671.

[339] Pangborn CA, Athanasiou KA. Growth factors and fibrochondrocytes in scaffolds. J Orthop Res 2005 Sep;23(5):1184-1190. DOI: 10.1016/j.orthres.2005.01.019

[340] Abbushi A, Endres M, Cabraja M, Kroppenstedt SN, Thomale UW, Sittinger M, et al. Regeneration of intervertebral disc tissue by resorbable cell-free polyglycolic acid-based implants in a rabbit model of disc degeneration. Spine 2008 Jun 15;33(14):1527-1532. DOI: 10.1097/BRS.0b013e3181788760

[341] Lippman CR, Hajjar M, Abshire B, Martin G, Engelman RW, Cahill DW. Cervical spine fusion with bioabsorbable cages. Neurosurg Focus 2004 Mar 15;16(3):E4. DOI: 10.3171/foc.2004.16.3.5

[342] Athanasiou KA, Niederauer GG, Agrawal CM. Sterilization, toxicity, biocompatibility and clinical applications of polylactic acid/polyglycolic acid copolymers. Biomaterials 1996 Jan;17(2):93-102. DOI: 10.1016/0142-9612(96)85754-1

[343] Heijkants RG, van Calck RV, De Groot JH, Pennings AJ, Schouten AJ, van Tienen TG, et al. Design, synthesis and properties of a degradable polyurethane scaffold for meniscus regeneration. J Mater Sci Mater Med 2004 Apr;15(4):423-427. DOI: 10.1023/B:JMSM.0000021114.39595.1e

[344] de Groot JH, Zijlstra FM, Kuipers HW, Pennings AJ, Klompmaker J, Veth RP, et al. Meniscal tissue regeneration in porous 50/50 copoly(L-lactide/epsilon-caprolactone) implants. Biomaterials 1997 Apr;18(8):613-622. DOI: 10.1016/S0142-9612(96)00169-X

[345] Grande DA, Halberstadt C, Naughton G, Schwartz R, Manji R. Evaluation of matrix scaffolds for tissue engineering of articular cartilage grafts. J Biomed Mater Res 1997 Feb;34(2):211-220. DOI: 10.1002/(SICI)1097-4636(199702)34:2<211::AID-JBM10>3.0.CO;2-L

[346] Funayama A, Niki Y, Matsumoto H, Maeno S, Yatabe T, Morioka H, et al. Repair of full-thickness articular cartilage defects using injectable type II collagen gel embedded with cultured chondrocytes in a rabbit model. J Orthop Sci 2008 May;13(3):225-232. DOI: 10.1007/s00776-008-1220-z

[347] Mizuno S, Glowacki J. Three-dimensional composite of demineralized bone powder and collagen for in vitro analysis of chondroinduction of human dermal fibroblasts. Biomaterials 1996 Sep;17(18):1819-1825. DOI: 10.1016/0142-9612(96)00041-5

[348] Glowacki J, Mizuno S. Collagen scaffolds for tissue engineering. Biopolymers 2008 May;89(5):338-344. DOI: 10.1002/bip.20871

[349] Walsh CJ, Goodman D, Caplan AI, Goldberg VM. Meniscus regeneration in a rabbit partial meniscectomy model. Tissue Eng 1999 Aug;5(4):327-337. DOI: 10.1089/ten.1999.5.327

[350] Bruns J, Kahrs J, Kampen J, Behrens P, Plitz W. Autologous perichondral tissue for meniscal replacement. J Bone Joint Surg Br 1998 Sep;80(5):918-923. DOI: 10.1302/0301-620X.80B5.8023

[351] Cook JL, Fox DB, Malaviya P, Tomlinson JL, Farr J, Kuroki K, et al. Evaluation of small intestinal submucosa grafts for meniscal regeneration in a clinically relevant posterior meniscectomy model in dogs. J Knee Surg 2006 Jul;19(3):159-167.

[352] Lumpkins SB, Pierre N, McFetridge PS. A mechanical evaluation of three decellularization methods in the design of a xenogeneic scaffold for tissue engineering the temporomandibular joint disc. Acta Biomater 2008 Jul;4(4):808-816. DOI: 10.1016/j.actbio.2008.01.016

[353] Hopkins RA, Jones AL, Wolfinbarger L, Moore MA, Bert AA, Lofland GK. Decellularization reduces calcification while improving both durability and 1-year functional results of pulmonary homograft valves in juvenile sheep. The Journal of thoracic and cardiovascular surgery 2009 Apr;137(4):907-913, 913e901-904. DOI: 10.1016/j.jtcvs.2008.12.009

[354] Aufderheide AC, Athanasiou KA. Assessment of a bovine co-culture, scaffold-free method for growing meniscus-shaped constructs. Tissue Eng 2007 Sep;13(9):2195-2205. DOI: 10.1089/ten.2006.0291

[355] Landesberg R, Takeuchi E, Puzas JE. Differential activation by cytokines of mitogen-activated protein kinases in bovine temporomandibular-joint disc cells. Arch Oral Biol 1999;44(1):41-48.

[356] Natoli RM, Responte DJ, Lu BY, Athanasiou KA. Effects of multiple chondroitinase ABC applications on tissue engineered articular cartilage. J Orthop Res 2009 Jan 2

[357] Bhargava MM, Attia ET, Murrell GA, Dolan MM, Warren RF, Hannafin JA. The effect of cytokines on the proliferation and migration of bovine meniscal cells. Am J Sports Med 1999 Sep-Oct;27(5):636-643.

[358] Vanwanseele B, Eckstein F, Knecht H, Stussi E, Spaepen A. Knee cartilage of spinal cord-injured patients displays progressive thinning in the absence of normal joint loading and movement. Arthritis Rheum 2002 Aug;46(8):2073-2078. DOI: 10.1002/art.10462

[359] Elder BD, Athanasiou KA. Synergistic and additive effects of hydrostatic pressure and growth factors on tissue formation. PLoS ONE 2008;3(6):e2341.

[360] Hall AC. Differential effects of hydrostatic pressure on cation transport pathways of isolated articular chondrocytes. J Cell Physiol 1999 Feb;178(2):197-204. DOI: 10.1002/(SICI)1097-4652(199902)178:2<197::AID-JCP9>3.0.CO;2-3

[361] Browning JA, Walker RE, Hall AC, Wilkins RJ. Modulation of Na+ x H+ exchange by hydrostatic pressure in isolated bovine articular chondrocytes. Acta Physiol Scand 1999 May;166(1):39-45. DOI: 10.1046/j.1365-201x.1999.00534.x

[362] Bonassar LJ, Grodzinsky AJ, Frank EH, Davila SG, Bhaktav NR, Trippel SB. The effect of dynamic compression on the response of articular cartilage to insulin-like growth factor-I. J Orthop Res 2001 Jan;19(1):11-17. DOI: 10.1016/S0736-0266(00)00004-8

[363] Buschmann MD, Gluzband YA, Grodzinsky AJ, Hunziker EB. Mechanical compression modulates matrix biosynthesis in chondrocyte/agarose culture. J Cell Sci 1995 Apr;108 (Pt 4):1497-1508.

[364] Kim YJ, Sah RL, Grodzinsky AJ, Plaas AH, Sandy JD. Mechanical regulation of cartilage biosynthetic behavior: physical stimuli. Arch Biochem Biophys 1994 May 15;311(1):1-12. DOI: 10.1006/abbi.1994.1201

[365] Torzilli PA, Grigiene R, Huang C, Friedman SM, Doty SB, Boskey AL, et al. Characterization of cartilage metabolic response to static and dynamic stress using a mechanical explant test system. J Biomech 1997 Jan;30(1):1-9. DOI: 10.1016/S0021-9290(96)00117-0

[366] Mauck RL, Soltz MA, Wang CC, Wong DD, Chao PH, Valhmu WB, et al. Functional tissue engineering of articular cartilage through dynamic loading of chondrocyte-seeded agarose gels. J Biomech Eng 2000 Jun;122(3):252-260. DOI: 10.1115/1.429656

[367] Nicodemus GD, Villanueva I, Bryant SJ. Mechanical stimulation of TMJ condylar chondro-cytes encapsulated in PEG hydrogels. J Biomed Mater Res A 2007 Nov;83(2):323-331.

[368] Darling EM, Athanasiou KA. Articular cartilage bioreactors and bioprocesses. Tissue Eng 2003 Feb;9(1):9-26. DOI: 10.1089/107632703762687492

[369] Martin I, Obradovic B, Treppo S, Grodzinsky AJ, Langer R, Freed LE, et al. Modulation of the mechanical properties of tissue engineered cartilage. Biorheology 2000;37(1-2):141-147.

[370] Gooch KJ, Blunk T, Courter DL, Sieminski AL, Bursac PM, Vunjak-Novakovic G, et al. IGF-I and mechanical environment interact to modulate engineered cartilage development. Biochem Biophys Res Commun 2001 Sep 7;286(5):909-915. DOI: 10.1006/bbrc.2001.5486

[371] Freed LE, Hollander AP, Martin I, Barry JR, Langer R, Vunjak-Novakovic G. Chon-drogenesis in a cell-polymer-bioreactor system. Exp Cell Res 1998 Apr 10;240(1):58-65. DOI: 10.1006/excr.1998.4010

[372] Naujoks C, Meyer U, Wiesmann HP, Jasche-Meyer J, Hohoff A, Depprich R, et al. Principles of cartilage tissue engineering in TMJ reconstruction. Head Face Med 2008;4:3.

[373] Adamopoulos O, Papadopoulos T. Nanostructured bioceramics for maxillofacial applications. J Mater Sci Mater Med 2007 Aug;18(8):1587-1597. DOI: 10.1007/s10856-007-3041-6

[374] Takigawa M, Okada M, Takano T, Ohmae H, Sakuda M, Suzuki F. Studies on chondrocytes from mandibular condylar cartilage, nasal septal cartilage, and spheno-occipital synchondrosis in culture. I. Morphology, growth, glycosaminoglycan synthesis, and responsiveness to bovine parathyroid hormone (1-34). J Dent Res 1984 Jan;63(1):19-22.

[375] Tsubai T, Higashi Y, Scott JE. The effect of epidermal growth factor on the fetal rabbit mandibular condyle and isolated condylar fibroblasts. Arch Oral Biol 2000 Jun;45(6):507-515. DOI: 10.1016/S0003-9969(00)00012-1

[376] Jiao Y, Wang D, Han WL. [Effects of various growth factors on human mandibular condylar cartilage cell proliferation]. Zhonghua Kou Qiang Yi Xue Za Zhi 2000 Sep;35(5):346-349.

[377] Fuentes MA, Opperman LA, Bellinger LL, Carlson DS, Hinton RJ. Regulation of cell proliferation in rat mandibular condylar cartilage in explant culture by insulin-like growth factor-1 and fibroblast growth factor-2. Arch Oral Biol 2002 Sep;47(9):643-654. DOI: 10.1016/S0003-9969(02)00052-3

[378] Delatte ML, Von den Hoff JW, Nottet SJ, De Clerck HJ, Kuijpers-Jagtman AM. Growth reg-ulation of the rat mandibular condyle and femoral head by transforming growth factor-{beta}1, fibroblast growth factor-2 and insulin-like growth factor-I. Eur J Orthod 2005 Feb;27(1):17-26. DOI: 10.1093/ejo/cjh068

[379] Ogawa T, Shimokawa H, Fukada K, Suzuki S, Shibata S, Ohya K, et al. Localization and inhibitory effect of basic fibroblast growth factor on chondrogenesis in cultured mouse mandibular condyle. J Bone Miner Metab 2003;21(3):145-153.

[380] Delatte M, Von den Hoff JW, Maltha JC, Kuijpers-Jagtman AM. Growth stimulation of mandibular condyles and femoral heads of newborn rats by IGF-I. Arch Oral Biol 2004 Mar;49(3):165-175. DOI: 10.1016/j.archoralbio.2003.09.007

[381] Yang H, Luo S, Li F, Zhou Z. [Study on IGF-I regulation the proliferation of rat condylar chondrocytes in vitro]. Hua Xi Yi Ke Da Xue Xue Bao 2000 Sep;31(3):365-366, 379.

[382] Suzuki S, Itoh K, Ohyama K. Local administration of IGF-I stimulates the growth of mandibular condyle in mature rats. J Orthod 2004 Jun;31(2):138-143. DOI: 10.1179/146531204225020436

[383] Song J, Luo S, Fan Y. [Effects of static tension-stress and TGF-beta 1 on proliferation of mandibular condylar chondrocytes]. Hua Xi Kou Qiang Yi Xue Za Zhi 2003 Feb;21(1):61-63, 73.

[384] Bailey MM, Wang L, Bode CJ, Mitchell KE, Detamore MS. A comparison of human umbilical cord matrix stem cells and temporomandibular joint condylar chondrocytes for tissue engineering temporomandibular joint condylar cartilage. Tissue Eng 2007 Aug;13(8):2003-2010. DOI: 10.1089/ten.2006.0150

[385] Hollister SJ, Levy RA, Chu TM, Halloran JW, Feinberg SE. An image-based approach for designing and manufacturing craniofacial scaffolds. Int J Oral Maxillofac Surg 2000 Feb;29(1):67-71. DOI: 10.1034/j.1399-0020.2000.290115.x

[386] Hollister SJ, Lin CY, Saito E, Lin CY, Schek RD, Taboas JM, et al. Engineering craniofacial scaffolds. Orthod Craniofac Res 2005 Aug;8(3):162-173. DOI: 10.1111/j.1601-6343.2005.00329.x

[387] Smith MH, Flanagan CL, Kemppainen JM, Sack JA, Chung H, Das S, et al. Computed tomography-based tissue-engineered scaffolds in craniomaxillofacial surgery. Int J Med Robot 2007 Sep;3(3):207-216.

[388] Chen F, Mao T, Tao K, Chen S, Ding G, Gu X. Bone graft in the shape of human mandibular condyle reconstruction via seeding marrow-derived osteoblasts into porous coral in a nude mice model. J Oral Maxillofac Surg 2002 Oct;60(10):1155-1159. DOI: 10.1053/joms.2002.34991

[389] Chen F, Chen S, Tao K, Feng X, Liu Y, Lei D, et al. Marrow-derived osteoblasts seeded into porous natural coral to prefabricate a vascularised bone graft in the shape of a human mandibular ramus: experimental study in rabbits. Br J Oral Maxillofac Surg 2004 Dec;42(6):532-537. DOI: 10.1016/j.bjoms.2004.08.007

[390] Srouji S, Rachmiel A, Blumenfeld I, Livne E. Mandibular defect repair by TGF-beta and IGF-1 released from a biodegradable osteoconductive hydrogel. J Craniomaxillofac Surg 2005 Apr;33(2):79-84.

[391] Weng Y, Cao Y, Silva CA, Vacanti MP, Vacanti CA. Tissue-engineered composites of bone and cartilage for mandible condylar reconstruction. J Oral Maxillofac Surg 2001 Feb;59(2):185-190. DOI: 10.1053/joms.2001.20491

[392] Abukawa H, Terai H, Hannouche D, Vacanti JP, Kaban LB, Troulis MJ. Formation of a mandibular condyle in vitro by tissue engineering. J Oral Maxillofac Surg 2003 Jan;61(1):94-100. DOI: 10.1053/joms.2003.50015

[393] Deng Y, Hu JC, Athanasiou KA. Isolation and chondroinduction of a dermis-isolated, aggrecan-sensitive subpopulation with high chondrogenic potential. Arthritis Rheum 2007 Jan;56(1):168-176. DOI: 10.1002/art.22300

[394] French MM, Rose S, Canseco J, Athanasiou KA. Chondrogenic differentiation of adult dermal fibroblasts. Ann Biomed Eng 2004 Jan;32(1):50-56. DOI: 10.1023/B:ABME.0000007790.65773.e0

[395] Safronova EE, Borisova NV, Mezentseva SV, Krasnopol'skaya KD. Characteristics of the macromolecular components of the extracellular matrix in human hyaline cartilage at different stages of ontogenesis. Biomed Sci 1991;2(2):162-168.

[396] Lindqvist C, Jokinen J, Paukku P, Tasanen A. Adaptation of autogenous costochondral grafts used for temporomandibular joint reconstruction: a long-term clinical and radiologic follow-up. J Oral Maxillofac Surg 1988 Jun;46(6):465-470. DOI: 10.1016/0278-2391(88)90413-2

[397] Yotsuyanagi T, Mikami M, Yamauchi M, Higuma Y, Urushidate S, Ezoe K. A new technique for harvesting costal cartilage with minimum sacrifice at the donor site. J Plast Reconstr Aesthet Surg 2006;59(4):352-359.

[398] Stockwell RA. The cell density of human articular and costal cartilage. J Anat 1967 Sep;101(Pt 4):753-763.

[399] Baek RM, Song YT. Overgrowth of a costochondral graft in reconstruction of the temporomandibular joint. Scand J Plast Reconstr Surg Hand Surg 2006;40(3):179-185.

[400] Samman N, Cheung LK, Tideman H. Overgrowth of a costochondral graft in an adult male. Int J Oral Maxillofac Surg 1995 Oct;24(5):333-335. DOI: 10.1016/S0901-5027(05)80484-9

[401] Barbero A, Grogan S, Schaefer D, Heberer M, Mainil-Varlet P, Martin I. Age related changes in human articular chondrocyte yield, proliferation and post-expansion chondrogenic capacity. Osteoarthritis and Cartilage 2004;12(6):476-484.

[402] Darling EM, Athanasiou KA. Rapid phenotypic changes in passaged articular chondrocyte subpopulations. Journal of Orthopaedic Research 2005;23(2):425-432.

[403] Isoda K, Saito S. In vitro and in vivo fibrochondrocyte growth behavior in fibrin gel: an immunohistochemical study in the rabbit. The American journal of knee surgery 1998;11(4):209-216.

[404] Schnabel M, Marlovits S, Eckhoff G, Fichtel I, Gotzen L, Vecsei V, et al. Dedifferentiation-associated changes in morphology and gene expression in primary human articular chondrocytes in cell culture. Osteoarthritis and Cartilage 2002;10(1):62-70.

[405] Hoben GM, Hu JC, James RA, Athanasiou KA. Self-assembly of fibrochondrocytes and chondrocytes for tissue engineering of the knee meniscus. Tissue Engineering 2007;13(5):939-946.

[406] Vanderploeg EJ, Imler SM, Brodkin KR, Garcia AJ, Levenston ME. Oscillatory tension differentially modulates matrix metabolism and cytoskeletal organization in chondrocytes and fibrochondrocytes. Journal of Biomechanics 2004;37(12):1941-1952.

[407] Johnstone B, Hering TM, Caplan AI, Goldberg VM, Yoo JU. In vitro chondrogenesis of bone marrow-derived mesenchymal progenitor cells. Experimental Cell Research 1998;238(1):265-272.

[408] Mackay AM, Beck SC, Murphy JM, Barry FP, Chichester CO, Pittenger MF. Chondrogenic differentiation of cultured human mesenchymal stem cells from marrow. Tissue Engineering 1998;4(4):415-428.

[409] Yoo JU, Barthel TS, Nishimura K, Solchaga L, Caplan AI, Goldberg VM, et al. The chondrogenic potential of human bone-marrow-derived mesenchymal progenitor cells. Journal of Bone and Joint Surgery - Series A 1998;80(12):1745-1757.

[410] Hwang NS, Varghese S, Zhang Z, Elisseeff J. Chondrogenic differentiation of human embryonic stem cell-derived cells in arginine-glycine-aspartate-modified hydrogels. Tissue Engineering 2006;12(9):2695-2706.

[411] Levenberg S, Huang NF, Lavik E, Rogers AB, Itskovitz-Eldor J, Langer R. Differentiation of human embryonic stem cells on three-dimensional polymer scaffolds. Proceedings of the National Academy of Sciences of the United States of America 2003;100(22):12741-12746.

[412] Schuldiner M, Yanuka O, Itskovitz-Eldor J, Melton DA, Benvenisty N. Effects of eight growth factors on the differentiation of cells derived from human embryonic stem cells. Proceedings of the National Academy of Sciences of the United States of America 2000;97(21):11307-11312.

[413] Wei ST, Yang Z, Liu H, Boon CH, Eng HL, Cao T. Effects of culture conditions and bone morphogenetic protein 2 on extent of chondrogenesis from human embryonic stem cells. Stem Cells 2007;25(4):950-960.

[414] Koay EJ, Hoben GM, Athanasiou KA. Tissue engineering with chondrogenically differentiated human embryonic stem cells. Stem Cells 2007 Sep;25(9):2183-2190. DOI: 10.1634/stemcells.2007-0105

[415] Khoo MLM, McQuade LR, Smith MSR, Lees JG, Sidhu KS, Tuch BE. Growth and differentiation of embryoid bodies derived from human embryonic stem cells: Effect of glucose and basic fibroblast growth factor. Biology of Reproduction 2005;73(6):1147-1156.

[416] Boon CH, Cao T, Eng HL. Directing stem cell differentiation into the chondrogenic lineage in vitro. Stem Cells 2004;22(7):1152-1167.

[417] Chen FH, Rousche KT, Tuan RS. Technology insight: Adult stem cells in cartilage regeneration and tissue engineering. Nature Clinical Practice Rheumatology 2006;2(7):373-382.

[418] Hoben GM, Willard VP, Athanasiou KA. Fibrochondrogenesis of hESCs: growth factor combinations and cocultures. Stem Cells Dev 2009 Mar;18(2):283-292. DOI: 10.1089/scd.2008.0024

[419] Hoben GM, Koay EJ, Athanasiou KA. Fibrochondrogenesis in two embryonic stem cell lines: effects of differentiation timelines. Stem Cells 2008 Feb;26(2):422-430. DOI: 10.1634/stemcells.2007-0641

[420] Zimmy ML. Mechanoreceptors in articular tissues. am J Anat 1988;182:16-32.

[421] Hills BA, Monds MK. Enzymatic identification of the load-bearing boundary lubricant in the joint. Br J Rheumatol 1998 Feb;37(2):137-142.

[422] Sindelar BJ, Evanko SP, Alonzo T, Herring SW, Wight T. Effects of intraoral splint wear on proteoglycans in the temporomandibular joint disc. Arch Biochem Biophys 2000 Jul 1;379(1):64-70. DOI: 10.1006/abbi.2000.1855

[423] Weasner Jr. JF. The determination of hydroxyproline in tissue and protein samples containing small proportions of this amino acid. Archives of Biochemistry and Biophysics 1961;93:440-447.

Biography

K. A. ATHANASIOU

K. A. Athanasiou is a Distinguished Professor and the Chair of the Department of Biomedical Engineering at the University of California Davis. He holds a Ph.D. in mechanical engineering (bioengineering) from Columbia University.

A. J. ALMARZA

A. J. Almarza is an Assistant Professor of Oral Biology and Bioengineering at the University of Pittsburgh and a faculty of the McGowan Institute of Regenerative Medicine and the Center for Craniofacial Regeneration. He is also the director of the Temporomandibular Joint Laboratory at the University of Pittsburgh. He holds a Ph.D. in bioengineering from Rice University and a post-doctoral fellowship at the Musculoskeletal Research Center of the University of Pittsburgh.

M. S. DETAMORE

M. S. Detamore is an Associate Professor of Chemical and Petroleum Engineering at the University of Kansas, where he is the director of the Biomaterials and Tissue Engineering Laboratory. He holds a B.S. in chemical engineering from the University of Colorado, and a Ph.D. in bioengineering from Rice University.

K. N. KALPAKCI

K. N. Kalpakci is performing his graduate studies at Rice University under the mentorship of Professor Athanasiou. The focus of his research is mechanical characterization and tissue engineering of the temporomandibular joint disc. He holds a B.S. in chemical engineering from the Colorado School of Mines.